LOVE & FURY

LOVE & FURY

The Magic and Mayhem of Life with Tyson

PARIS FURY

HODDER &
STOUGHTON

First published in Great Britain in 2021 by Hodder & Stoughton
An Hachette UK company

1

Copyright © Paris Fury 2021

A CIP catalogue record for this title is available from the British Library

Hardback ISBN 978 1 529 34619 0
Paperback ISBN 978 1 529 34620 6
eBook ISBN 978 1 529 34621 3

Typeset in Celeste by Hewer Text UK Ltd, Edinburgh
Printed and bound in Great Britain by Clays Ltd, Elcograf S.p.A.

Hodder & Stoughton policy is to use papers that are natural, renewable
and recyclable products and made from wood grown in sustainable
forests. The logging and manufacturing processes are expected to
conform to the environmental regulations of the country of origin.

Hodder & Stoughton Ltd
Carmelite House
50 Victoria Embankment
London EC4Y 0DZ

www.hodder.co.uk

CONTENTS

This book is dedicated to my other half, my partner in crime, my biggest nightmare and dream-come-true all in one man: my husband Tyson. I look forward to our next chapters . . .

PROLOGUE

WHEN PEOPLE ASK me how it feels to be married to Tyson Fury, I tell them it's like a rollercoaster ride: full of ups and downs and twists and turns, with a few scares and thrills along the way. There's never been a dull moment, that's for sure.

Tyson's boxing success has given me a fantastic lifestyle – I've travelled the world, and I'm surrounded by lots of nice things – but there have been times in my marriage when fame and fortune have meant nothing to me. Behind closed doors my life hasn't always been a bed of roses, and with the magical highs have come some miserable lows.

When I first fell in love with Tyson, aged just sixteen, I had no idea what the future held. All I'd ever wanted from life was a happy home and a big family, and to be a good wife and mother. But within a few years I'd not only become the wife of the heavyweight champion of the world, but also the wife of a person suffering with severe mental illness.

When Tyson and I took the joint decision to open up about his struggle with depression and my experience of living with a sufferer, I started to see how widespread this issue is. So many partners are supporting their loved ones through similar situations, as well as raising families, and this reality has encouraged me to tell my story, as frankly and honestly as possible. It's not only about the crazy, funny, sometimes infuriating, sometimes nail-biting side of my amazing life with Tyson but also what it's been like to support him through addiction and depression.

When your partner is in crisis, things can seem really overwhelming, especially when you have children to bring up and a household to run. Often you don't know what to do, where to turn or who to talk to. Sometimes you feel your whole world is crumbling but, as the backbone of the family, you're expected to stay strong for everyone. And, as you try to cope with the pressures of daily life, you can feel terribly isolated, like you're the only person experiencing this living nightmare.

To those of you who are going through a similar experience: you're not alone. I've been there too and I know how you feel.

I'm so proud of my husband for being open and honest about the demons he's fought and the challenges he's faced, and for raising awareness of mental health. But there's another side of the story: my side. I want to give a voice to everyone out there who, in the face of adversity, tries their best to support the family, hold things together and maintain some kind of normality.

Whatever your own experience of love and life, I hope this book strikes a chord. Writing it has reminded me that, when times get rough, you can dig deep and find an inner strength. And, not only can you pull yourself through, you can emerge all the tougher for it. I've learned that, no matter how desperate you feel, there's always some hope to cling onto. So don't ever give up. Sometimes you have to go through the darkness to find the light.

CHAPTER ONE

MY GYPSY CHILDHOOD

I SOMETIMES WONDER where I get all my strength from – I've needed tons of it while living with Tyson, let's face it – and I reckon it's mostly down to my upbringing. I come from a long line of Scottish Gypsies, a heritage I'm very proud of, and I spent a very happy childhood at Tilts Farm, a Travellers' site in South Yorkshire. I learned most of my life lessons from my mam, Lynda, who brought me up to respect our community's customs and traditions, and who taught me the skills and principles that would shape me as a person. She was – and still is – a really wise, caring and resilient woman and, like many mothers, she became the 'glue' that bonded our family together.

Mam spent most of her early life roaming around America with her parents and seven siblings, and met my dad, Jimmy Mulroy – a fellow Scottish Traveller, who worked in the antiques trade – when her family returned to the UK in the late 1970s. When Mam became pregnant with their first child, my sister Romain, my parents upped sticks and towed their trailer down from Newcastle-upon-Tyne, where they'd initially settled as newlyweds. With a baby on the way, Mam wanted to be closer to her relatives – Tilts Farm was a regular stop-off for her brothers and sisters – and they thought it would be an ideal place to bring up a young family.

'Tilts', as everybody called it, was (and still is) situated in Tollbar – a small village near Doncaster – and was surrounded by acres of woods, fields and farmland. Running through the middle of the three-acre site was a long tarmac road, which was flanked by rows of concrete bays that housed caravans and trailers of all shapes and sizes. Each individual plot had its own wash shed, too. Tilts was a privately owned stopping place, as opposed to a council-run transit site, which meant that once people had their pitch there, they stayed for months or years rather than days or weeks. The sense of permanence made it an extremely friendly site. At any one time there could be up to a hundred trailers and caravans pitched up, but you'd still get to know all the various families dotted around the area, from the Wilsons in the middle of the site to the Blairs at the back end. In fact, you'd often discover that you were somehow related to many of your fellow residents, which wasn't massively surprising, considering that the Traveller community only makes up a tiny percentage of the UK population.

Family values ran deep at Tilts Farm. Many generations lived side by side, from great-grandparents down to great-grandchildren, and everyone looked after and watched over each other. Our elders were cherished and respected, and were cared for by relatives; no one would ever dream of

putting them in rest homes. At the other end of the age spec-
trum, babies and youngsters were a real source of pride.
Raising sons and daughters was seen as the finest gift of all
among the Gypsy community, and it wasn't unusual for
families to have four or five kids in tow; the more, the merrier.

In common with many Traveller sites, Tilts relied upon a
huge network of trust. Knowing everybody on the site,
directly or indirectly, created a real sense of safety and
security. If a child went to play with a new friend in another
trailer, for instance, their mother either knew the family in
question very well or, on the rare occasion she didn't, would
have a word with a relative or a neighbour beforehand, just
for reassurance.

'Who's in the Hobby trailer that's just pulled on?' she'd
ask, if some new residents had arrived. 'D'you think my
Rosie would be OK with them?'

'Yeah, that's my sister-in-law and her family,' her friend
would reply. 'They're all good people. She'll be looked after,
don't worry.'

That sense of familiarity – the known rather than the
unknown – was a cornerstone of Traveller life. It felt really
comforting to be surrounded by people from your own
community, who shared a similar outlook and background
to your own.

The Tilts network had its practical uses, too. If you wanted
your broken window fixing, a neighbour would point you in
the direction of the best handyman in the business, who
lived in the trailer two rows down. If you needed a birthday

cake, an aunt might put you in touch with her oldest friend, a talented baker who made the finest chocolate sponge on site. If anyone needed any clothes making or altering they'd often come knocking on Mam's door. She was a really arty and creative person who could knock up anything on her sewing machine, from cushion covers to christening gowns. And if a neighbour wanted to buy a wedding ring or a Wedgwood vase they'd speak to my dad, who dealt in jewellery and antiques and owned a shop in Doncaster town centre. Tilts people were very kind and considerate; lots of good deeds were done, and many favours were returned.

My parents' firstborn, my sister Romain, arrived in 1985. She had a pretty tough start in life, unfortunately. At just six weeks old, she contracted whooping cough – a fairly common but highly contagious bacterial disease – and spent a lot of time in and out of Doncaster Royal Infirmary. Romain's case was more severe than most, sadly, and led to serious breathing difficulties that ultimately and tragically caused damage to her brain. Doctors advised my parents that her physical capabilities were likely to be unaffected – she'd still be able to walk and talk – but they wouldn't be able to assess the full extent of any learning disabilities for a good few years.

As Romain grew older, her behavioural differences became more apparent – she didn't interact and communicate in the same way as other children in her friendship group – and, as she reached primary school age, her emotional development seemed to stall. During a hospital appointment Mam and Dad were given the sad news that, in all likelihood, their daughter would forever have the mental capacity of a five-year-old.

My parents were naturally upset about Romain's situation, but from the outset – and to their credit – they just accepted the card they'd been dealt. They adapted to her needs and challenges, of course – my mother was especially devoted to her, and still is – but they chose neither to give her a label nor wrap her in cotton wool.

'Romain is Romain,' Mam would say, keen to raise her as normally as possible. 'I want people to treat her like any other child.'

My brother Jimmy – my parents' only son – was born in 1986, and I came along three years later, in 1989. There's no doubting that Jimmy would have much preferred a little brother to play with – he was a typical rough-and-tumble lad, who loved toy cars, ball games and rolling around in the dirt – but instead he got landed with a pink, fluffy girly-girl who treasured her Barbie dolls and her Fisher-Price tea sets.

Jimmy and I spent most of our early years bickering with one another, but things calmed down in 1992 following the birth of our little sister. Montana and I were completely different; she was a proper tomboy and, unsurprisingly, had much more in common with my brother. While I stayed inside our trailer, dressing up in Disney princess costumes and wobbling around in Mam's stilettos, the other two would be roaming around outside in their tracksuits and trainers. However, although my younger sister and I weren't natural playmates, we rarely fell out. Despite our chalk-and-cheese personalities, we loved each other dearly.

As children go, Jimmy, Montana and I were pretty well-behaved and rarely crossed the line with Mam and Dad. Their parenting style was quite strict – they wouldn't stand for any fibs, cheek or backchat – so we knew where our boundaries lay, and tended not to push our luck. We were aware that Romain needed a large amount of my parents' attention, too – rightly so – and we didn't want to cause them any more trouble than necessary. Like most Travellers we were also raised in the Roman Catholic faith. As the Holy Bible said, we were expected to 'Do unto others as you would have them do unto you' by treating people with kindness and respect.

On reflection, having a sister with disabilities helped me to grow up faster, I think, certainly in comparison with other children my age. Because of Romain I knew that life wasn't always plain sailing, and that challenges could appear just when you least expected them. She also gave me a great lesson in the value and importance of family loyalty. By supporting and protecting each other, I saw how a tight-knit unit could overcome any hurdle or obstacle.

'Always stick up for your sister, Paris,' Mam would say, aware that other kids would sometimes poke fun at her strange behaviour.

'I will Mam, I promise,' I'd reply. I was true to my word. If any other child dared to be mean to Romain, or complain about her presence, they'd get short shrift from me.

'Paris, does your sister *have* to play with us?'

'Yes, she does. If *she* doesn't play, then *I* don't play.'

Traveller kids didn't generally participate in organised activities in the 'outside world' – ballet classes and rugby clubs weren't our thing – but we occupied ourselves in different, perhaps simpler ways: riding our bicycles, making dens and playhouses, and exploring the local countryside. Many Tilts lads got into boxing, which had always been popular within male Gypsy circles, and which went right back through the generations. I wasn't in the least sport-minded, so I paid no attention to the fights and fisticuffs that took place in and around the site. If only I'd known then what I know now. I'd have never guessed that, in years to come, boxing would play such a huge part in my own life.

While some Traveller families chose to move from site to site, the Mulroy clan was quite happy to remain in one place, for a couple of reasons. For Romain, who regularly attended a nearby special school, it gave her much-needed routine and stability in her life. And Dad had no plans to venture further afield, since his antique shop had become very well established in Doncaster. In bygone times, Gypsies including my ancestors would have roamed around the country in their horse-drawn carts and caravans to seek work, constantly moving their wives and kids from one stopping place to another in order to find jobs.

'A going foot always gets something, even if it's a blister,' as my Granny Mary used to say. But our lifestyle has changed a great deal since then.

Our plot at Tilts Farm was larger than many of our neighbours' since it had to accommodate a number of separate units. My parents slept in their own big 24-foot trailer. Their bedroom was an explosion of colour (it had a huge floral bedspread with matching cushions and curtains) and their lounge looked like a miniature museum, with all their wedding heirlooms proudly on display. Travellers loved their ornaments and collectables – things like sterling silver dishes and crystal glass decanters – yet they preferred to polish and cherish these possessions, as opposed to actually using them.

Mam worked hard to keep their trailer looking immaculate. It was like a show home. She'd clean it, shine it and tidy it to perfection, before locking the door and pocketing the key.

'Now you mustn't go in there, children,' she'd say, wagging her finger at the four of us. 'I've got it looking spotless, and I don't want anyone inside.'

'But what's the point of making it look nice if no one can see it?' I'd ask, puzzled by her logic.

My sisters and I had the adjacent caravan to ourselves, a small Hobby tourer. The storage cupboards were jam-packed with our favourite items – books, games, clothes, make-up – and it felt like our own cosy little sanctuary, somewhere we could chat and chill out together, in private. As regards sleeping arrangements, the caravan had a double bed at either end and a bunk bed in the middle, but Romain, Montana and I would often choose to snuggle up together at night-time. All three of us hated sleeping alone.

The Portakabin next door housed Jimmy's bedroom, in addition to our communal living and dining space. The lounge boasted a giant flat-screen TV and, in common with many Gypsy households, all the chairs and sofas were covered in sheets of clear, protective plastic to keep them in pristine condition. The adjoining kitchen was a hive of activity – Mam would rustle up a hearty meal for six each night, usually traditional fare like hotpot or shepherd's pie – and the food cupboards were always full of treats and snacks. The Portakabin became our little social hub where we'd gather to eat, chat, play games and watch movies. We weren't the kind of children who hid away in our bedrooms every night, glued to our Game Boys and PlayStations; we genuinely enjoyed our family time together.

Some parts of the trailers were out of bounds, however. In keeping with Gypsy tradition, we chose not to use our indoor bathrooms. Because the shower and toilet cubicles were so near to the cooking and eating areas, Travellers considered it unhygienic to use them – or to launder clothes and tea-towels in the kitchen – so we'd head outside to our purpose-built wash block instead. Anyone unfamiliar with our community might have found this ritual quite strange, but it was an age-old part of our culture that we became totally accustomed with. The four Mulroy kids got used to waiting their turn in the bath shed queue; it certainly hardened us to the elements, especially in the middle of winter.

'Hurry up, Jimmy, you've been ages . . .' I'd whine, shivering in my dressing gown with a rolled-up towel clamped under my arm.

'Hang on, I'm nearly done,' he'd say.

Occasionally my family enjoyed a change of scenery from Tilts Farm. At least every other weekend we'd visit my Mulroy granny and grandad, who lived in a large house in Bedlington, near Newcastle-upon-Tyne. There, we'd meet up with Dad's four siblings – Aunt Janey, Uncle Tommy, Aunt Molly, Aunt Sally and their respective children – with each family occupying one bedroom. It was chaos – there were cousins all over the place, and the noise levels were crazy – but I thought it was brilliant. I loved being part of these big, boisterous get-togethers.

In the summertime we'd pitch up to our favourite Travellers' gathering. Based in the Scottish Borders, the annual St Boswells Fair attracted thousands of visitors, who came from far and wide. It was just one of a network of fairs across the UK that, in line with a long-standing Gypsy tradition, acted as a trading post for the menfolk – they'd buy and swap livestock, machinery and precious metals – and boasted rows of stalls, aimed largely at the women, that sold clothes, crafts and china. In spite of its name there was no actual fairground, but the Mulroy kids would be quite happy wandering around the site with our cousins, or sitting around a campfire while the grown-ups enjoyed a sing-along. Travellers loved the opportunity to belt out a good tune. Any of the old classics would do the trick for my family, from the Beatles to the Bee Gees.

I considered myself fortunate to have a foreign holiday every summer, too. My mam needed her annual sunshine fix and would whisk us all off to the Canary Islands for a fortnight. These trips abroad were far from fancy (they were usually package holidays booked with a high street tour operator) but Mam always reckoned it was money well spent.

'It probably costs me less to take you to Tenerife than it does to take you to Scarborough,' she'd say with a smile. 'And this way, I can get myself a suntan, too.'

My father never came with us, though. He was a proper homebody who wasn't keen on hot weather or overseas travel, so Mam would often invite her youngest sister (my Aunt Romain) to come along, as well as her children. We cousins usually stuck together, splashing in the swimming pool by day and dancing at the kids' disco by night . . . the usual Brits abroad stuff.

Mam's zest for life was incredible – it still is – and, when we were young, she'd always ensure there was something marked on the calendar to look forward to. She saved up to take us on yearly coach trips to Disneyland Paris (such a magical experience) and, back home in the UK, we'd spend fun-packed days out at Camelot Theme Park in Lancashire, or the coastal resort of Skegness. Wherever we went you could guarantee loads of laughs and lots of larking around. She was such a fantastic mother. Not only did she keep all four of us entertained, she also cared for us so brilliantly, particularly Romain, who to this day still lives with Mam and Dad. She was totally devoted to making our childhood as happy and as stable as possible, and I'll forever be thankful for that.

*　　*　　*

There still exist lots of myths around Gypsies and learning. Some people assume that we're totally uneducated, but that's not always the case. My parents were very keen that I went to school to learn the basics, and from the age of four I began attending our local village school, Arksey Primary. I was one of only three Traveller children in my class, although I wasn't aware of any barriers between me and the Gorger kids ('Gorger' being our commonly used – and respectful – term for non-Gypsies). I never got any sense from the teaching staff that I was different, and I certainly never felt any pressure to stick with my own kind. From my first day onwards I was made to feel very welcome, and I settled into my primary school routine straight away.

My teachers included Mrs Cartwright (strict), Mrs Grey (kind) and Miss Hartley (my favourite). The last was a well-spoken former opera singer in her sixties who was obsessed with spelling, grammar and pronunciation.

'Miss *Har-T-ley*!' she'd scold if any pupil dared to miss out the 'T' in her surname. 'In this class we sound *each letter . . .*'

I clung on to her every word – I'd try hard to say 'think' instead of 'fink' and 'right' instead of 'reet' – and her passion for the English language really stayed with me. Even now, my friends will jokingly accuse me of 'talking posh' – they reckon I use too many long, complicated words – and I'm convinced that's due to Miss Hartley's influence. Not only that, whenever I find myself nagging my own children about their lazy speech, I can still hear my teacher's voice echoing in my head.

I was a hard-working and well-behaved pupil at Arksey – I don't once remember being told off, or being sent to the headmaster – and, without blowing my own trumpet, I was put on the top table for most subjects. Although I fared pretty well with reading and writing (and managed to get by with art and science) it was maths that I really excelled in. I loved number-crunching and problem-solving and was particularly good at mental arithmetic, which came in handy whenever I watched Channel 4's *Countdown* after school. I'd be glued to the telly as Carol Vorderman selected the contestants' numbers ('two from the top, Carol, and four from the bottom . . .') prior to Richard Whiteley starting the *Countdown* clock. I'd then attempt to calculate the sum in thirty seconds – I'd add, subtract, divide and multiply in my head without the need for pen and paper – and more often than not I'd arrive at the correct answer. But while I totally smashed the numbers round ('Aren't you clever, Paris!' Mam would say) I was completely useless when it came to the words section. I rarely got anything more than four letters long.

Anti-Traveller incidents at Arksey Primary were few and far between, thankfully. A minor kerfuffle once took place when a classmate called me a 'gypsy' in the playground – it was intended as an insult – but that was swiftly nipped in the bud.

'Don't be so unkind,' he was told by a dinner lady, who ordered him to apologise immediately.

'Rude people like that are best ignored,' said Mam when I returned home from school that afternoon, feeling a little hurt. 'Be proud of who you are, Paris, and don't listen to anyone who suggests otherwise.'

Another episode saw a teacher assuming I couldn't tell the time, implying it was beyond the intelligence of a young Traveller kid. She was quite taken aback when I proved her wrong, correctly identifying the position of the big hand and the little hand, just like my mother had taught me.

Like most Gypsy children, however, I stopped attending mainstream school when I was eleven. In the eyes of my community Arksey Primary had served its purpose, since I'd been taught the basics of reading, writing and arithmetic. As was our custom, it was time for me to return to the family fold to commence a different kind of education, just like my parents before me, and my grandparents before them. Instead of going to high school I'd remain at home, embarking upon an alternative type of learning journey that would not only teach me more about the Traveller culture – how to observe our values, how to preserve our traditions – but would also equip me with practical, hands-on skills in preparation for life as an adult.

'It's important to learn *our* ways before we learn the world's ways,' I remember being told by an elder. 'There are plenty of people who can pass exams, Paris, but who can't change a nappy or replace a wheel. Intelligence takes many different forms . . .'

As far as I was concerned, bypassing high school wouldn't hamper any future ambitions or aspirations that I might have. GCSEs and A levels weren't the be-all and end-all. My chosen path may have been out of the ordinary but, in my mind, it wouldn't prevent me from succeeding in life. Not that my formal education was completely grinding to a halt, in any case. Doncaster Council organised twice-weekly classes at a local community centre, specifically aimed at Traveller kids like me, that offered tutoring in IT, maths and literacy. Further down the line we'd also receive careers guidance and expert advice with regard to learning a trade, finding a profession or accessing a college course.

So, from summer 2000 onwards, Mam took me under her wing. More often than not we were alone together, because Jimmy spent most days working with Dad in the shop, Romain continued to attend her special school and Montana was still being taught at Arksey Primary.

'OK, Paris, let's get up, let's get ready, and let's get moving,' my mother would say with a smile, before preparing our breakfast and switching on the TV for half an hour or so.

We led a very active life, busying ourselves with a variety of daily tasks. One morning Mam would show me how to polish her precious collection of ornaments – she was very fond of her china dolls set – and the next she'd teach me how to wash the family laundry without the fabric shrinking or the colours running. Sometimes I'd try my hand at deep-cleaning the carpets, disinfecting the surfaces or doing some outdoor DIY.

'It's all about presenting your home as nicely as you can, Paris,' Mam would say, making me aware that I'd be follow-ing in her footsteps one day. 'Always make sure that every-thing is sparkling.'

Travellers were very proud, upstanding people – appearances and reputations mattered a lot – and it was vital that those standards never slipped. Running a successful household was a true badge of honour.

My mother and I would chat constantly as we tackled our daily chores, and I'd love listening to stories about her own eventful childhood. Mam and her siblings – she was the eldest of eight kids – spent much of their youth shuttling between Scotland, England and America. Their father, Johnny Marshall, was a building contractor who journeyed far and wide to find work, and the family constantly moved between towns and cities, pitching up at stopping places along the way. When Mam was in her mid-teens my grandad taught her how to drive a truck, so she could tow one of their two caravans along smaller roads and busy freeways. She was more than happy to do her bit, as were her brothers and sisters.

'Family life is all about mucking in and sticking together, Paris, through the good times and the bad,' Mam would tell me. 'Things can fall apart if you don't.'

These words of advice would stick in my mind, for use at a later date.

My mother would also tell me about the years she spent in Las Vegas, where the Marshalls were based in the mid-1970s. The city had built itself a reputation as the showbiz capital of the world, and as a teenager Mam was lucky enough to see Elvis Presley, the Osmonds and the Jackson 5 performing at the height of their success. In what became her proudest boast, however, she was able to watch my Granny Mary give a palm reading and a crystal ball reading to Liberace, the famous pianist with the flashy lifestyle. Like many women of Gypsy heritage, Mary had a gift for fortune-telling and was much sought after in VIP circles.

'I can't quite remember what she predicted for Liberace,' Mam told me, 'but I can still picture his mansion in Vegas. I'd never seen anything so amazing in my life.'

I'd always been a bit of a mammy's girl, but spending so much time in each other's company definitely brought us closer together. That being said, my mother and I weren't confined to the home 24/7; that would have driven her totally mad. She liked to get out and about, and she'd vary our routine with trips to the local swimming pool, or outings to Meadowhall shopping centre in Sheffield. We'd also plan lunch dates with Mam's friends (who'd often bring along their own daughters) and would also pay visits to various family members in the area.

Now and again I was allowed to spend the day working with Dad in his shop. Located on a Doncaster high street, it sold a wide selection of jewellery and antiques and attracted a steady stream of buyers and browsers. I spent most of the time answering the telephone or serving customers, like a proper employee, and really enjoyed observing how to run a business and how to deal with clients.

'So who's this new assistant of yours, Jimmy?' a shopper would say as I carefully wrapped up their antique vase in tissue paper. 'She's doing a grand job.'

'This is my daughter, Paris,' my father would say, smiling. 'She's going to be a top saleswoman one day.'

For a young girl, I was already pretty savvy. Dad had agreed to pay me a wage of £20 per day but, on top of that, I'd also negotiated myself a ten per cent sales commission. My maths skills often came in handy when I totted up my earnings.

'Hey Dad, I think you'll find that it was *me* who sold that silver bracelet today, not you,' I'd say as I examined the contents of my pay packet. 'You owe me another fiver . . .'

When I was about eleven years old, Mam and Dad took the difficult decision to leave Tilts Farm. While they were very fond of the place – we'd spent ten happy years there by then – they were keen to move somewhere more permanent, and liked the idea of getting a foot on the property ladder. They certainly weren't alone in wanting a more settled existence; it had become quite common for Gypsy families to swap their trailers for houses as they sought extra comfort and convenience in their lives.

My parents found a three-bedroom semi-detached house in the village of Bentley, just a mile or so down the road from Tollbar. It was probably less spacious than our sprawling plot at Tilts – my sisters and I had to share a fairly small room, not that we were complaining – but we all grew quite fond of our new home. There were elements of the old site that we missed, of course – the constant buzz of activity, the close network of neighbours, that wide circle of trust – but moving to Bentley just seemed the right move at the right time. Leaving the Tilts community didn't mean that we'd deserted our culture and tradition. Anything but. Our living arrangements may have changed, but our Traveller identity had not.

I continued to hook up with my friends at weekends but, as we got older, many of the girls wanted to expand their horizons. They'd ask their parents to drop them off at the Dome – a leisure complex in Doncaster that housed an ice rink, a swimming pool and a number of restaurants – but I wasn't always keen to join them. I was quite a home-bird – I much preferred to stay indoors, watching *Friends* with my sisters or tackling one of my puzzle books – and I was also still very shy. Believe it or not, I was quite socially awkward in my early teens and, unlike my pals, found it tough to mix and mingle. I never knew quite what to say in a group conversation – small-talk didn't come easily to me – and I'd often find myself holding back instead of holding forth. I was particularly coy when it came to boys. In fact, up until the age of fifteen I can safely say that I had no interest in the opposite sex whatsoever.

'See that lad over there, Paris? He keeps looking over at you,' a friend would whisper as we enjoyed a milkshake in McDonalds. 'Why don't you give him a smile back?'

'Don't be daft,' I'd say, as my cheeks burned. 'Anyway, he's probably staring at you, not me . . .'

Looking back, this was probably the Mulroy half of me emerging, since my dad's family were, on the whole, pretty quiet and reserved. In contrast, many of Mam's relatives were big personalities, and definitely weren't backward in coming forward. That Marshall confidence would rub off on me eventually, but it would take a good few years before it did.

I did like going to the cinema, though. While I wasn't that bothered about typical teenage hobbies like pop music or video games, I loved to take in a good movie and had a serious crush on Josh Hartnett, the handsome American actor who played the role of Danny in one of my favourite films, *Pearl Harbor*.

It was during one such cinema trip, when I was about thirteen, that I found myself on the receiving end of some anti-Traveller prejudice. Three of us were approaching the ticket desk of our local multiplex in Doncaster one Saturday afternoon, all really excited at the prospect of some film and popcorn action, when we were stopped in our tracks.

'No Travellers,' said the bloke at the counter, shaking his head.

'I beg your pardon?' I asked, taken aback.

'Travellers are banned from coming in today. Sorry.'

'But we've been here loads of times before, and—'

The man turned away and walked off before I could finish my sentence, leaving my friends and me in total shock. *How could he be so rude? What had we done to deserve this? And, more to the point, how the heck did he know we were Travellers?* We could only assume that he had some kind of inbuilt Gypsy radar.

Mam didn't take it lying down when I returned home and told her what had happened. She was furious and got straight on the phone to the cinema, telling them in no uncertain terms how disgusting their attitude was, how appallingly they'd treated three respectable teenage girls and how guilty they were of serious discrimination. She didn't buy their explanation – that a group of trouble-causing Travellers had forced them to take these measures – so she drove us both down there to demand some straight answers.

'Here she is,' said my mother, presenting me to the red-faced manager. 'Tell me here and now that this girl – *my daughter* – has ever behaved badly in your cinema.'

'Er, no, I can't say that she has,' he muttered. 'I can only apologise to you both, madam, and try to assure you that this will never happen again . . .'

But it did. It wouldn't be the first time, or the last, that my friends and I would be treated like second-class citizens.

Not everyone in my home town treated Travellers with such disrespect, though, and when I applied to Oracle Training College in 2004, to study for a National Vocational Qualification in Beauty Therapy, I was welcomed in. I almost fell into it by accident. A year or so previously, during one of the council-run Traveller education sessions, I'd been allowed to choose an additional subject from a list that included construction, cookery and beauty. Building walls and baking cakes didn't really float my boat, but messing about with hair and make-up sounded OK, so I gave it a whirl. To my surprise I found I was pretty good at it, and – with Mam and Dad's blessing – I decided to sign up for the three-year NVQ college course.

There was one stumbling block, though. Being fourteen, I was a year too young to enrol at Oracle, since applicants had to be fifteen or above. However, I was so keen to get going that I decided to turn up to the registration day regardless. I'd simply convince the staff that I had the talent and determination to secure a place, in spite of my age.

Right, so what kind of outfit does a college girl wear? I remember thinking to myself on the morning of the open day, before selecting a pair of smart black trousers and a pink jumper from my wardrobe. I applied some light make-up, tied my hair back into a ponytail and checked out my reflection in the mirror. I definitely looked older than my years – I was quite tall, and could have easily passed for eighteen – and I figured I wouldn't look massively out of place. I grabbed the folder I'd bought the previous day – I reckoned it would make me look more studious – and, after kissing Mam goodbye, I headed over to the college. It was perhaps the first time in my life that I'd felt a proper flush of confidence.

I stayed for the entire open day, totally fascinated by all the talks and demonstrations. I had a long chat with a beauty therapy tutor – a lovely Canadian called Sharon – who said I'd be well-suited to the course, before asking if she could see my CV.

'But it says here that you're only fourteen!' she said, scanning my personal details.

'Yes, but I'm good enough,' I replied. 'Isn't that just as important?'

'I'm afraid it doesn't quite work like that, Paris,' she said with a smile. 'Come back in six months. We'll keep your place warm.'

She kept her word and, once I'd turned fifteen, I was welcomed back to college. I loved the course from the outset, whether it was learning about business accounting or being taught how to do the perfect pedicure. And, despite being the youngest student in a group of twenty, I managed to work my way up to the top of the class. Beauty therapy just seemed to come naturally to me, both practically and theoretically.

I think my tutors, Sharon and Paula, were pleasantly surprised by my progress. They were well aware of my education history – they knew I'd left school at eleven – and were at first worried I might struggle to cope in this new learning environment.

'Considering you've never written an essay before, Paris, this is fantastic,' I remember Sharon saying after a tutorial, handing over my coursework with a big red 'A' scrawled on the front. 'You're really very talented, and I can't help but wonder what you might have achieved if you'd gone to high school. You could have easily become a writer or something.'

I'm sure she intended this as a compliment, and I was pleased to hear it, but I also felt a little put out. I'd always been satisfied with the route I'd chosen, and didn't like the implication that I'd been disadvantaged in any way, or prevented from reaching my full potential.

'To be honest, Sharon, I think the reason I'm so free-thinking is because I *didn't* go to secondary school,' I replied, eager to stand up for myself. 'I reckon formal education might have knocked that creativity out of me, and might have even changed me as a person.'

'D'you really think so?'

'Yeah, I do. I don't think it would have been the right path for me at all.'

'Fair enough, Paris,' she said, shrugging her shoulders. 'All I can say is keep up the good work. You're doing brilliantly.'

'I will. Thank you.'

I passed my NVQ course with flying colours, achieving my Grade III certificate a year ahead of schedule. I was snapped up as an apprentice by one of the most reputable beauty salons in the area – Blush, in the village of Sprotbrough – and was paid a wage of £200 per week, plus commission for any treatments that I was qualified in, like facials and pedicures. That salary felt like a fortune to me.

I really enjoyed my job. I loved my newfound independence, I loved having a sense of purpose and I loved doing something that I excelled in. And, to add to my general happiness with life, I'd just started dating the most amazing young man.

CHAPTER TWO

MEETING MY MATCH

THE FIRST TIME I caught sight of Tyson Fury, in the summer of 2005, I couldn't help but laugh. I was with Mam, my Aunt Mandy and her daughter Maria – we'd just arrived at a hotel in Nottingham, having travelled over from Doncaster for a friend's wedding – and as we walked through the car park we noticed a huge, hulking man trying his best to heave himself out of the passenger seat of a Mercedes. He was a tangle of knees and elbows, with a mop of dark curly hair, big bushy sideburns and a long frizzy beard.

'Hey, look at Farmer Giles over there,' chuckled Maria as we walked past. 'Shall we ask him if he needs any help?'

'Nah, I think he'll manage,' I said, smiling, before heading to the neon-lit main entrance and greeting the smartly dressed doorman.

A couple of hours later, with the party in full swing, a familiar face waved at us from across the room and made a beeline for our table. The Traveller community was so close-knit that whenever a wedding took place – no matter which part of the country – you'd never fail to bump into people you knew really well. In this case it was Aunt Theresa, a sixty-something family friend. We called most of our parents' pals Aunt or Uncle, even if they weren't blood relations.

'You look lovely, Paris,' she said with a smile, giving me a hug and a kiss on the cheek. 'And what a pretty outfit.'

Mam had bought me a new aqua and black suit for the wedding - a jacket and a skirt – which I'd topped off with a wide-brimmed aqua hat. I was wearing my waist-length blond hair loose and, since it was a special occasion, I'd carefully applied some Rimmel Sunshimmer bronzer and some Lancôme Juicy Tube lipstick.

'Thank you,' I replied. 'You look lovely, too, Aunt Theresa.'

'Come over here with me.' She beckoned to me. 'There's someone I'd like you to meet.'

Oh yeah, I think I know what's happening here, I thought to myself. Ladies like Aunt Theresa loved nothing more than matchmaking at social gatherings, and she'd have been fully aware that, at the ripe old age of fifteen, I'd never had a proper boyfriend. My shyness had probably been a factor, although I was slowly starting to come out of my shell, particularly since I'd begun my college course in Doncaster.

Lots of women in our community settled down quickly – many got married before they were twenty – and, in Aunt Theresa's eyes, it was probably high time I was paired off. Linking my arm, she led me through the crowd of wedding guests to a young man standing in the hotel lobby, and tapped him on the back. This fella was far too tall to be tapped on the shoulder.

'This is my nephew,' she said, beaming. 'Tyson, I'd like to introduce you to this lovely young lady. I've known Paris since she was a tiny baby and, as you can see, she's grown into a really beautiful girl.'

Well, this is a bit embarrassing, I thought, as I felt my cheeks reddening. *And who exactly is this lad, anyway?*

Barely able to see out of my flying-saucer-shaped hat, all I could make out was a broad torso in a smart shirt and over-coat. But as I tilted my head up to get a proper look at his face, I soon realised I was staring at the bearded, curly-haired man I'd seen struggling to get out of his car. My God, this bloke was *huge* – his head was only inches away from the ceiling – and I couldn't help but wonder why Aunt Theresa had earmarked somebody who appeared to be a decade older (and a foot taller) than me.

'Well go on then, say hello to her,' cajoled our go-between.

'Hello,' he said.

'Hello,' I replied, shyly.

After a few seconds of awkward silence – I sensed Aunt Theresa willing her nephew on – he gave me a brief nod and turned away, leaving me to just wander back to my table. I didn't give this Tyson bloke a second thought – he clearly had zero interest in me – and I spent the rest of the evening getting down on the dancefloor (minus the big hat, of course). Nothing would have suggested that I'd just met the man who was going to become my husband and soulmate.

A few months after the Nottingham wedding, I was enjoy-ing an evening out in Doncaster town centre with a group of friends. I'd bought myself a new pair of thigh-high leather boots, which I'd teamed with some jeans and a crop-top, and I was pretty happy with the way I looked and with life in general. We were heading to a local youth centre – a place where we could grab a game of pool and a Coca-Cola – when one of the lads I was with, Owen James, pointed and yelled something about spotting his cousin, and sprinted off in the direction of a nearby takeaway joint. We followed him in – a few of my pals fancied a snack-stop – and standing at the counter, ordering a supersized kebab, was Tyson. All six feet something of him.

It's that bloke from the wedding, I said to myself. *Aunt Theresa's nephew.*

'Hello again,' he said smiling, looking me up and down. 'Nice boots.'

I assumed that he was taking the mickey, so I decided to throw back some shade. Sporting a baggy pair of army print combats teamed with a khaki jumper made him a pretty easy target, to be fair.

'Nice trousers,' I countered. 'Where d'you get those beauties from?'

'Oxfam.' He laughed. 'You got a problem with that?'

As we waited for our orders, we chit-chatted for a few minutes. Tyson explained he'd travelled over from Manchester with his brother to visit a poorly aunt. He also told me he was an amateur boxer, following in the footsteps of his father John who was now training him. But nothing about that impressed or surprised me, because I knew plenty of Traveller lads who were into boxing. My jaw hit the floor, though, when he said he'd just turned seventeen years old.

Seventeen, seriously? Only two years older than me? I'd honestly thought he was about twenty-five.

I left the kebab shop feeling strangely drawn to this Mancunian man-mountain. He was much more handsome than I'd remembered – he'd ditched the straggly beard and bushy sideburns – and he'd made me laugh a couple of times as we'd buzzed off each other. I'd definitely sensed a little spark between us.

'So who was that old fella you were talking to, Paris?' asked my friend Maria as we stepped back out onto the pavement.

'Well, he's not old, as it happens, and his name is Tyson.' I smiled. 'Tyson Fury.'

I celebrated my sixteenth birthday in December 2005, and had planned a full schedule of activities to mark the occasion. The day would kick off with an afternoon trip to the cinema to watch *The Exorcism of Emily Rose*, and would be followed by a limousine ride into Doncaster for a dance and a few soft drinks until the strict 10 p.m. curfew that Mam had imposed. A sleepover at home with a handful of girl-friends would cap off my special day.

News of my plans soon spread among the local Traveller community – we rarely refused a chance to party – and, unbeknown to me, word had even reached Manchester. An amateur boxer called Hosea Burton (who most knew as

'Othea') had got wind of some girl's birthday bash in Doncaster and just happened to mention it to his cousin Tyson. The lure of the boxing gym was always stronger for Tyson, even at the weekend, but – after some arm-twisting – he had agreed to drive over with Othea just to keep him sweet. It was only when they finally arrived in the town centre that Tyson realised that the birthday girl was me.

'Well I never, it's *you*,' he said, smiling, as he approached our group.

'Yes, it is,' I replied. 'You can wish me happy birthday if you like.'

'Oh yeah, sorry. Happy birthday.'

'Thanks very much.'

Just as I was wondering whether fate was playing a part in these chance meetings, my phone rang. It was Mam, asking me and my friends to pop home for the all-important Mulroy family ritual of cutting my birthday cake. I was going to have to head off home for an hour. Tyson seemed slightly put out – he teased me for being greedy by not sharing my cake – and I found myself asking him and Othea if they wanted to join us.

'You can even give us a lift to my place if you like,' I said.

'All right, then,' Tyson replied. 'It'd be my pleasure.'

My boldness was extremely out of character (I could see my friend giving me a side-eye as if to say *Paris, you hardly know him!*) but I felt guilty that Tyson and his cousin had travelled all that way. I double-checked with Mam, who said she didn't mind them tagging along.

Othea drove us the couple of miles to my place, Tyson sitting in the passenger seat and my friend and me in the back. The banter flowed, much of it initiated by the loud and lively Tyson, and it all seemed very relaxed and natural. It felt quite exciting being in the company of these two strapping lads from Manchester.

'Has anyone ever said you look like a Sindy doll?' said Tyson at one point, as he turned round to stare at my poker-straight blond hairdo. He may have intended it as a compliment, but I certainly didn't take it that way.

'Sindy was a second-rate Barbie, I think you'll find,' I replied, glaring at him. I'd always been Team Barbie as a young girl; in my view, she had tons more glamour than boring ol' Sindy.

When Othea pulled up to the house, Mam was standing at the front door to greet us. She smiled when she saw Tyson.

'Hi there. I've been waiting for you to come over,' she said with a wink, before ushering us all into the lounge, where all my family were waiting.

What did she mean by that? I wondered to myself.

I couldn't help but notice that Tyson's brashness and bravado ebbed away when we arrived at my place. After posing for a few jokey photos with me, he spent the following half-hour slumped on the sofa, barely saying a word as the conversation flowed around him. It was as if a switch had been flicked inside his head, like he'd gone from social butterfly to shrinking violet. It was such a difference in attitude and was quite strange to witness. I didn't know him well enough to ask him what the matter was – maybe this big family gathering was a little intimidating – so I just left him alone.

Once I'd been treated to a chorus of 'Happy Birthday' (and had blown out my sixteen candles) I headed back into Doncaster with my girlfriends, travelling in style via a shiny stretch limo. Tyson and Othea followed in the car behind us. Sadly, however, our attempt to get into a local cafe-bar was kiboshed. My pals and I just wanted a good dance – we weren't bothered about drinking alcohol – but as some of us were under eighteen, the whole group was refused entry.

So with nowhere to go and party – and not wanting to risk anywhere else – my friend and I ended up sitting in the car with Tyson and Othea again, chatting to them until curfew-time. Tyson had perked up, thankfully, and judging by all the eye contact and cheeky smiles I sensed he'd taken a bit of a shine to me. The feeling was mutual. There was just something about him that I really liked. There was a connection.

While there was no kissing or smooching (in our community, any physical contact with a boy was frowned upon until you were officially 'going out' together), Tyson did pluck up the courage to ask for my number before we parted company. And I was more than happy to oblige. He was probably the first boy I'd ever felt a spark of attraction with.

The following day I quizzed my mother about the remark she'd made to Tyson as he'd walked through the door.

'What was all that about, Mam?'

'I knew you'd ask me that,' she said with a smile. 'I caught him staring at you when we were at that wedding in Nottingham, and I just had a feeling I'd be seeing him again.'

She didn't miss a trick, my mother.

The following week I was quite chuffed to receive a flurry of calls and texts from Tyson, which all followed a similar theme.

'Paris, when I next come through,' (the Traveller way of saying 'visit') 'will you go out with me?'

I'd been brought up to expect that the boy always pursued the girl, never vice versa, and at first I decided to play it cool. Plus, the idea of him being my very first boyfriend was a really big deal and I needed to be sure I was doing the right thing.

'I don't think so, Tyson, I barely know you,' I replied, prompting him to text me the same question again . . . and again . . . and again. Fair play to the lad, he was persistent.

While I'd enjoyed our little game of cat and mouse, there came a point when I couldn't resist any longer and, just prior to Christmas 2005, I agreed to a meet-up. Tyson suggested that we both go to the local cinema one Friday evening to see the recently released remake of *King Kong*. I felt a real buzz of excitement as his car drew up to the house that night to pick me up. As he opened the passenger door for me he gave me a lovely wide grin, and my heart melted.

Even before the film's opening credits had started to roll I'd officially agreed to be his girlfriend – Tyson seemed thrilled – and then the pressure began to mount for The First Kiss. I'd never snogged a boy before – I was quite the innocent – and as the lights went down in the auditorium I felt my heart pounding and my palms sweating. It was the longest film ever – over three hours long – and for every one of those minutes I was frozen to the seat, knowing at some point Tyson would seize his moment. It didn't come until the very last scene. Just as King Kong was clambering up the Empire State Building, Tyson leaned over to make his move, only for me to burst out laughing.

'I don't know what I'm supposed to do,' I giggled nervously. 'I've never kissed anyone before.'

'Don't worry,' my brand new boyfriend whispered. 'I'll teach you.'

I found out later that within days of our first date, Tyson had told both his mother and father that he'd met the girl he was going to marry. While they were glad to see him so upbeat, they'd apparently not taken him too seriously.

My family were pleased that we were properly courting; they'd become very fond of Tyson and were happy I'd paired up with a fellow Traveller. It was important to them that we'd be sharing similar values, morals and life experiences and, if we happened to stick together, we'd be passing our culture down to the next generation.

Not all relationships were confined to the Gypsy community, of course. Most young people I knew were free to date Gorgers if they wished, but those who did could end up drifting away from Traveller life, and there was always the risk of diluting or losing many long-held, much-loved traditions. So, while there was no such thing as an arranged marriage within my circle, plenty of 'elders' did their utmost to fix up Traveller boys and girls.

'Don't you think the Smiths' daughter and the Lees' son would make a lovely couple?' you'd hear them say. 'Shall we try and set them up?'

Once we'd officially become an 'item', Tyson came over to Doncaster as often as he could. Traveller tradition put the onus on the boys to visit the girls, not the other way round – 'if they want you, they'll come and get you,' as my granny used to say – so it was a while before I'd meet the Fury family, who lived in the village of Styal, on the outskirts of Manchester.

Tyson would either pick me up from Mam's house or meet me outside Oracle College where, in the early days of our relationship, I was nearing the end of my beauty therapy course. Much to his embarrassment, I'd often drag him into my classroom to act as one of my models. We had to practise beauty treatments on real people in order to pass our NVQ so it was often a question of grabbing whoever was available.

'Oh my God, is he your boyfriend?' a fellow student whispered to me the first time Tyson walked in, looking really muscly in his jeans and T-shirt. 'He's so *buff*...'

Poor Tyson would then have to sit patiently in the treatment area as I gave him a facial or a pedicure, once even painting his fingernails.

'You'd better make sure you clean this off properly, Paris,' he warned as I applied a bright shade of fuchsia, adding a sprinkling of glitter. 'My life won't be worth living if the lads in the gym see it.'

'Can you just keep your hands still, please?' I snapped. 'If I smudge the edges, I'll fail my module.'

Once I'd completed my course and started work at the Blush salon, to my surprise I found myself earning more money than Tyson. He wasn't making much at all from amateur boxing, of course, and relied on a variety of labouring jobs: roof-tiling, tree-cutting, patio-laying; any manual work that might pay him thirty quid here or fifty quid there. Occasionally he'd lend a helping hand to his dad, John, who bought and sold cars for a living.

Any spare cash that Tyson had was spent filling up his petrol tank to get him to Yorkshire and back. If he ever wanted to stay overnight he'd have to kip in the little visitors' caravan that was pitched outside Mam and Dad's house. Sex before marriage was widely discouraged in our community – that was the Travellers' way – and we were both happy to behave ourselves. This situation chimed with our religious beliefs, too. Since childhood, both Tyson and I had been brought up to be God-fearing Catholics. He was very frank and open about his love of God – he spoke freely about his spiritual relationship with Him – and he gained a great deal of comfort from saying his prayers and reading the Holy Bible. Compared with Tyson I had a more private approach to my faith, but I shared his devotion to it.

As the weeks passed, I realised I was growing very fond of Tyson. Not only was he tall, dark and handsome, I also loved his caring nature and his sense of humour. I was really enjoying having a boyfriend in my life – it was all quite new to me – but I still had no idea if it would turn into something meaningful. There's no denying that I felt very safe and 'looked after' with him at my side; put it this way, no one in their right mind would get on the wrong side of Paris Mulroy knowing her other half was Tyson Fury.

Sometimes his mood could be a little hard to gauge, though. On the outside, and in public, he displayed all the cockiness and swagger you'd expect from a budding boxer and streetwise Mancunian Traveller. But on the inside – and in private – he was extremely shy and reserved, vulnerable even. He could retreat into his shell for no apparent reason – as I'd noticed on my sixteenth birthday – and sometimes almost shut down, unable and unwilling to engage. It was puzzling, but I became used to his mood swings and just saw them as part of his unique, unpredictable nature.

Sometimes I even found myself having to give my boyfriend extra encouragement to carry himself with more confidence. Being freakishly big and brawny for a teenager made him quite self-conscious about his height.

'You're slouching again, Tyson,' I'd whisper whenever I caught him hunching his shoulders. 'Walk tall, why don't you? Hold your head up high.'

When it came to spending time together on day trips and nights out, Tyson and I tended to keep things simple. We'd both been raised in modest homes, without much money sloshing around. One of our favourite pastimes was to go skating at Doncaster Dome ice rink. For a huge, hulking bloke in size 12 skates, Tyson was surprisingly agile on the ice, even if he did have to be ultra-cautious when a boxing bout was looming.

'What if I fall and twist my ankle?' he'd say as we stepped onto the ice. 'My trainer will kill me.'

'You'll be fine. Just take it slow and cling on to me,' I'd say, grabbing his arm. He'd then skate off, showing the kind of balance you wouldn't have expected from someone his size.

In spring, when the weather improved, we'd head to the countryside for some fresh air. More often than not we'd drive over to Cusworth Hall, a Georgian country house surrounded by beautiful parkland, where we'd sit on a hill with a picnic and enjoy the views across the South Yorkshire valleys. We'd chat about our family, our friends – our life in general – and found that we shared similar opinions about lots of things. Sometimes we'd talk about the future; I'd bounce around the idea of starting up my own beauty salon business, and he'd tell me all about his hopes and dreams as a boxer.

'I'm going to be heavyweight champion of the world one day, just you wait and see,' he'd say with a grin.

'There's nothing wrong with aiming high,' I'd reply.

But, in all honesty, I never took Tyson's claims of world domination seriously. Even though I could see he was doing well on the local amateur circuit, I just assumed his boxing was a passing phase. I reckoned he'd eventually lose interest in fighting – like many of his Traveller counterparts – and would put down his gloves, quit the sport for good, and continue with the tree-felling and the car dealing to earn a decent, regular income.

Some weeks Tyson would drive over to treat me to lunch or dinner, and we would usually end up in one of the cheap 'n' cheerful chains. Neither of us were much interested in fancy foods or swanky restaurants; in fact, one of our earliest dates took place at the Doncaster branch of Frankie & Benny's. I still cringe at the memory of the fool I made of myself. I'd never eaten Italian food before (well, it was Italian-*ish*) and, as I ran my finger down the laminated menu, I decided on a tasty-sounding dish called spaghetti carbonara.

The minute the plateful of pasta arrived I realised I'd chosen the worst possible date-night meal. I had no idea how to eat this worm-like pasta covered in creamy gloop, so – petrified that I'd slop it down my new top – I just pushed it around my plate. No wonder Tyson raised his eyebrows at my untouched meal; to him, this faddy eating was a serious waste of his hard-earned cash.

But date nights out were pretty rare in the early days of our romance, since I often found myself playing second fiddle to Tyson's boxing commitments. I couldn't fault his dedication to the cause, but it didn't do wonders for our social life. He'd spend most Friday and Saturday nights either sparring in the gym or fighting in the ring, which often left me attending parties and get-togethers on my own. I felt annoyed at his priorities and took it all very personally, frequently giving him grief for choosing his sport over his girlfriend.

'Why don't you want to come to the races with me?' I'd yell down the phone. 'You're a young man, Tyson, you should be going out and enjoying yourself, not stuck inside a sweaty gym all day and night.'

'Sorry, Paris, it's the way it has to be,' he'd reply, sticking firmly to his guns.

Me turning up to events and parties alone, like Billie-No-Mates, would sometimes prompt my friends to joke about this imaginary boyfriend of mine.

'So are we ever going to meet this Tyson fella?' they'd ask, tongues firmly in cheek. 'In fact, does the guy even *exist*?'

'He's training for a big fight, if you must know,' I'd say defensively, as my pals comically rolled their eyes.

Now, of course, I wonder why I hassled him so much, but at the time I didn't understand the true extent of my boyfriend's ambition and didn't appreciate his willingness to make sacrifices.

As time went on, though, the penny dropped that the easiest way for me to see Tyson at weekends was to attend one of his fights; it was a case of if you can't beat 'em, join 'em. The very first bout I watched took place in nearby Sheffield, where he was often based with the England amateur boxing squad. I felt quite curious to see what this other side of his life was all about. Sitting alone in the crowd, that evening I witnessed my boyfriend being applauded into the ring, looking fabulous in his red and black vest and shorts, with his shiny gloves and his protective headgear.

Wow, my boyfriend is a proper boxer . . . I remember thinking to myself as the reality finally dawned on me. *This is more than just a hobby* . . .

As the countdown to the fight progressed, my nerves began to jangle. This was a whole new experience for me and I really didn't know what to expect, or how I'd react when the fight started. Tyson seemed to ooze with confidence, though, as he bounced on his toes in preparation. From my ringside perspective, not one single ounce of him appeared worried that he'd lose, or frightened that he'd get hurt. His self-belief was incredible.

As soon as the bell ding-dinged for round one Tyson sprang into action, and the outcome was just obvious. As he prowled around the ring and pummelled his opponent, even a first-time spectator like me could see that there was only one victor. He was masterful. He was in his element. I almost felt sorry for the hapless challenger in the opposite corner as he crashed to the deck and clung to the ropes.

There was a real buzz around Tyson afterwards, with all his fans and spectators queuing up to tell him that he was the real deal, the next big thing.

'Now d'you believe me, Paris?' he joked as he signed a few autographs. 'Your boyfriend is going to be the future heavyweight champion *of the world* . . .'

The media was now taking a real interest in him too. An article in the *Manchester Evening News* described this up-and-coming boxer as having 'male model looks with a gentle, shy manner' and a television camera crew trailed after him for a couple of days. Tyson was keen to save as much memorabilia as possible, so I started to keep a folder of all the press cuttings as well as videotaping all his TV appearances.

As proud as I was of Tyson's talent – and as keen as I was for him to be a success – it still didn't make me a massive fan of boxing, and my support in those days was more dutiful than pleasurable. I watched most of his northern-based fights (Mam wouldn't allow me to travel further afield) and, while it was great to witness him in action, doing what he did best, I still wasn't fazed by the whole experience. I certainly wasn't one of those adrenalin-pumped girlfriends who'd shout and scream each time their partner landed a punch; on the contrary, I'd just sit quietly in my seat, privately willing Tyson to win the fight (which he invariably did), to do himself justice, and to avoid getting hurt. Nowadays, with the stakes much higher and the opponents more fearsome, I do get quite emotionally involved – and very stressed out – but that's not how it was then.

Tyson continued to do well, losing only four of his thirty-five amateur boxing matches. On the rare occasions he did lose, he'd often head straight up to me in Doncaster. I was impressed with how well he coped with defeat – he was quite matter-of-fact about it – but he always preferred to make a quick getaway to escape all the post-fight debriefs and inquests. Chilling out with me he could forget about boxing for a while, and the Mulroy family home became his little sanctuary.

Very occasionally I'd go along to Tyson's midweek training sessions, which took place in a tiny backstreet gym in the Manchester suburb of Wythenshawe. One time, as I watched a female fighter shadow-boxing in the ring, Tyson chucked me a pair of gloves.

'Go and have a spar with her, she won't mind,' he said.

'I'm not really sure, Tyson . . .' I replied – I wasn't a very sporty person – but then the girl beckoned me over with a friendly smile and I felt obliged. I pulled on some gym gear, tied my hair back and climbed into the ring. But as soon as I saw her whacking her gloves together and flexing her bulging biceps, I quickly chickened out.

'Erm, d'you mind if we do some skipping instead?' I asked, as I heard Tyson chuckling in the background.

'Yeah, sure,' she said, laughing, taking off her gloves and handing me a rope.

It was the spring of 2008, and we were just enjoying one of our lunchtime picnics at Cusworth Hall when Tyson laid out his plans to me for the year ahead.

'So here's what's happening, Paris,' he declared. 'Firstly, I'm going to fight at the European Championships. Then I'm going to compete at the Beijing Olympics. After that I'm going to win the English title. And then I'm going to marry you.'

I almost couldn't speak. This had come as a big surprise. He may not have gone down on bended knee – it was more of a statement of fact than a romantic proposal, like he was pencilling in a diary entry – but I felt so thrilled to hear those words. I said yes straight away. The idea of spending our whole life together as man and wife, perhaps bringing up a family of our own, made me feel so happy. For the next few days I floated on air, barely able to suppress my ear-to-ear smile. *Tyson Fury wants to MARRY ME!*

Our families were delighted when we told them our plans; my mam, with her sixth sense, told me she'd seen it coming, and my dad and siblings were very pleased for us both. By then I'd met Tyson's parents, John and Amber – two really nice people, who made me feel very welcome – as well as his elder brother John Boy, who'd already left home, and his younger brothers, Shane and Hughie. I got to know Shane better than anyone else; he was closest in age to Tyson and would often drive over to Doncaster with him, hooking up with his Yorkshire-based pals while his brother and I spent time alone. Shane and his girlfriend Helen got married around the same time as us – we had kids at similar stages, too – and we all became very close.

My future father-in-law expressed some concerns that the wedding build-up might distract Tyson from his fight preparations, but I assured him it wouldn't. Mam and I would be doing the lion's share of the planning and organising, and would be pulling out all the stops to make it a real day to remember. Tyson – like many grooms-to-be, I suspect – was more than happy to leave us to it, although he did agree to arrange our wedding-night hotel.

'I'll find us somewhere really special, my darling,' he said with a wink.

The date was set for Friday 21 November 2008, fitting in with Tyson's mad-busy boxing schedule and working around his summer trip to China. Mam and I viewed and booked the Stables in nearby High Melton for the big day, a beautiful venue that specialised in staging fairy-tale winter weddings.

I started to attend fittings for my white off-the-shoulder bridal gown, which was being hand-made by a specialist dressmaker in Lincolnshire. It was inspired by Julia Roberts' character in *Runaway Bride.*

'Whenever I get married, *that's* the dress I want,' I'd said as a young girl, when I'd watched the film with Romain and Montana. Now, almost a decade later, my dream was coming true.

We'd also started to think about our first home. Traditionally for us, the husband-to-be and his side of the family were expected to buy the newly-weds' property – usually a caravan or a trailer – while the in-laws would buy all the interior furnishings and equipment, from pots and pans to curtains and cushions.

But then our schedule was thrown into the air when Tyson's plan to attend the Beijing Olympics fell through. He was absolutely shell-shocked. Another fighter, the more experienced David Price, had been chosen to represent Great

Britain instead and Tyson's Plan B – to compete for Ireland by gaining citizenship through his family's Galway and Tipperary roots – didn't come together in time.

Quickly seeing an opportunity to turn a disaster into an advantage, Tyson insisted we get hitched in the summer instead. Adding to his sense of urgency was the fact he'd now found and bought a brand new trailer that we could move into straight afterwards.

'But Tyson, it's too late to change the date,' I argued. 'The Stables wouldn't be able to rearrange things at such short notice, and you know I've got my heart set on a winter wedding. Also, if we cancelled we'd lose our deposit, and we can't afford to do that.'

'Aw, c'mon, Paris, let's just go for it,' he moaned. 'I've got the whole summer free now. Why wait until November?'

My fiancé clearly didn't understand the amount of planning and organisation that went into a wedding. I was beginning to realise how incredibly impulsive he was, the sort of person who lived life in the moment and liked to make decisions on the hoof. In Tyson's world, our big day could be rescheduled on a whim, just like one of his boxing matches. I was having none of it, though, and refused point blank to change the date.

He wouldn't let the matter rest, though – he was like a dog with a bone – and that spring we squabbled constantly. As tensions simmered between us I soon found myself reaching breaking point – it was one conflict after another – and, after an ugly slanging match with him outside Mam's house,

I decided to call time on the wedding *and* our relationship. He thought I was joking when I dropped the big bombshell, then he realised I was deadly serious. I simply couldn't take any more, I told him. As far as I was concerned, we were done. Our courtship was over.

Tears were streaming down my face when I broke the bad news to Mam. While she put on the kettle and made a cup of tea – the usual British way of handling a crisis – I asked her to go ahead and cancel the wedding as I couldn't face doing it myself.

'Leave it to me, Paris,' she said. 'I'll sort things out, don't you worry.'

'Thanks, Mam,' I sniffled.

For the next six weeks, other than a few tetchy text messages, Tyson and I steered well clear of each other. I continued enjoying nights out in Doncaster with the 'young company' (what Travellers called their group of similarly-aged friends) and did my utmost to move on from the disappointment of our break-up. I'd been brought up to have a positive, pragmatic outlook – 'there's no point in dwelling on the past' was a common family saying – and I would, forgive the boxing analogy, take it on the chin. Our relationship clearly wasn't destined to be a forever thing, I told myself, and Tyson evidently wasn't cut out to be my husband. While I would learn a lot from the experience of Boyfriend #1, as far as I was concerned it was onwards and upwards. I'd dust myself down and pick myself up, no problem.

My pals were keen to get the low-down on the big split –
most of them thought we were a match made in heaven – and
I had to explain that things hadn't worked out for us, sadly,
and that it was just another case of young love turning sour.

The realisation that our relationship was possibly beyond
repair came a few months later, when I heard on the grape-
vine that Tyson had travelled to Ibiza for a lads' summer
holiday. To me, that spoke volumes. No sooner had we split
up than he was off gallivanting abroad, no doubt larking
around with other girls. So I was taken aback when – just
after he'd returned to the UK – he sent me an emotionally-
charged text. He told me he couldn't believe I'd abandoned
our relationship so easily, and he couldn't bear the thought
of me meeting somebody else. He ended the message by
warning me that if I ever got married, he'd turn up to the
church to halt the ceremony.

I was furious. *You creep,* I said to myself as I deleted the
message. *Talk about having your cake and eating it. How
dare you . . .*

A week or so later, I was getting ready for a trip to York
Racecourse with my pals (going to the races was always one
of my favourite days out) when Tyson unexpectedly called
me up, asking if he could tag along.

'Don't bother,' I said, still feeling very hurt and upset. 'You
just carry on with that single life of yours.'

He was there at the racecourse when I arrived, though,
and flashed me a big smile as I walked in. Deep down I was

pleased to see him too, but I was determined not to let it show. I purposely avoided him for an hour or so, but when we finally caught up with each other it was obvious the chemistry still existed between us. Despite everything that had happened, he still made my heart skip a beat.

As we sat together in the stands, watching the horses galloping past, Tyson revealed his true feelings. He told me that, in his mind, our relationship had never really ended, it had just been put on hold for a while. He appreciated we'd needed some breathing space after our bust-up, but he felt we'd be mad to throw in the towel. By the end of the conversation I found myself agreeing with him. We kissed and made up, and decided to let bygones be bygones.

'Shall we make a new start?'

'OK. Let's give it a go.'

What followed was our own little Summer of Love. Tyson's omission from the Olympics had freed up more time in his schedule for us to be together and, keen to take full advantage of this, I did something quite daring: I quit my job at Blush. While I knew I'd miss working in the beauty salon – and would definitely miss my weekly wage – I was willing to give it all up if it meant salvaging our relationship. We whiled away our days lazing on Skegness beach or hiking in the Yorkshire Dales and, as we chatted from sunrise to sunset, we learned so much more about one another. Our love just grew stronger and we both realised that, while neither of us were perfect, we were perfect for each other. We were meant to be.

With our wedding plans firmly back on track, it was time to have a conversation with my mother.

'Mam, I'm really sorry for messing you about, but I think we might need to re-book the Stables,' I said.

Much to my surprise, she gave me a broad smile.

'No need, Paris,' she said. 'I never cancelled it in the first place. I knew you and Tyson would patch things up in the end.'

On a chilly November afternoon, just a few weeks shy of my nineteenth birthday, we finally became husband and wife. We were both keen to have a traditional religious wedding and we exchanged our vows and rings at St Peter-in-Chains Roman Catholic Church in Doncaster.

We invited three hundred friends and relations to the reception (Tyson couldn't understand why we weren't able to have more; I think he wanted to invite half the population of Manchester) and, while it was a big Gypsy wedding, it wasn't quite on the same scale as a certain reality show. The marquee at the Stables was given a winter wonderland theme – lots of ice-blue, white and silver – and was beautifully illuminated with candles and chandeliers. The wedding breakfast was amazing (Tyson had requested his favourite apple crumble for dessert) and the evening entertainment came courtesy of a great singing duo who belted out a medley of dancefloor fillers. It was such a happy, joyous occasion.

Tyson and I left our own party fairly early, bidding a fond farewell to our guests at about 10 p.m. We hailed a taxi into

Doncaster and, as we cosied up together in the back seat, I wondered exactly where we'd be spending our first night as Mr and Mrs. That decision had been left up to Tyson, of course; it was the only wedding-related task he'd been given.

Imagine my surprise, then, when my husband led me through the entrance of a town centre hotel, strode up to the reception, rang the bell and asked the girl at the desk if he could reserve a room for the night. I couldn't believe what I was hearing.

'You've not booked a room, Tyson?' I hissed. 'It's our flamin' wedding night!'

'I forgot – sorry – but I'm sure they'll be able to sort us out,' he replied with a shrug. 'Chill out, Mrs Fury . . .'

Charming, I remember thinking. *I've landed myself a right Casanova here, haven't I?*

Goodness knows what the receptionist thought of these two daft, disorganised newly-weds, but fortunately she was able to fit us in. Had the hotel been full, no doubt we'd have spent our first night together in the Travelodge on the M18 motorway.

The following day, Tyson and I headed to the Algarve for our honeymoon. His aunt and uncle had kindly organised it for us, and had asked us to choose our resort. We'd opted for a destination with as short a flight time as possible, since Tyson had only recently returned from a tournament in the US and didn't fancy any more time on a plane.

For some reason I'd imagined that Portugal was going to be red hot in November (geography was never my strong point) so I'd packed my suitcase with a selection of floaty dresses and skimpy bikinis. I soon discovered that the Atlantic coast was anything but tropical at that time of year.

'Doncaster's probably warmer than this place,' I moaned, as the wind rattled against our hotel room window. 'It's bloody freezing . . .'

'It's not cold, Paris, it's mild,' said Tyson, but that was only because he'd just returned from a five-mile run along the beach.

As it happened, our Algarve trip only lasted four days instead of the planned fortnight. The honeymoon had coincided with Tyson's decision to turn professional, a development that had been on the cards for a while. Not only had the Olympics situation hurt him deeply, having set his heart on winning a gold medal, but he'd also become pretty disillusioned with the world of amateur boxing. He reckoned he'd been the victim of some dubious results – rounds and bouts he'd clearly dominated had been awarded to opponents – and, on top of this, he suspected that he'd occasionally been a victim of racial stereotyping. Traveller boxers were all too often pigeon-holed as rough-and-ready street-fighters and, in his opinion, weren't afforded the same respect as others.

'They won't give me a chance, Paris, they won't let me progress. It's time to move on,' he kept saying. 'I might as well get punched in the face and get paid for it, rather than getting punched in the face for a plastic cup.'

Forsaking his amateur status in order to turn pro was an inevitability, but it had arrived earlier than planned; talks had been ongoing with a number of boxing promoters, but everything finally came to fruition while we were in Portugal. The professional contract had to be signed sooner rather than later, and I remember poring over the paperwork in our hotel room before emailing it over to his new promoter, Mick Hennessy. The business accounting module that I'd studied at college came in very handy sometimes.

A fight was lined up for Tyson straight away. It would feature on the same bill as high-profile middleweight Carl Froch, and would also be televised live on ITV. However, as it had been scheduled to take place at the Nottingham Arena on Saturday 6 December, we'd need to fly home immediately so Tyson could start training.

'I'm really sorry about this,' he said, worried I'd be cheesed off about our short-lived honeymoon.

'It's fine, I totally understand,' I replied. 'It's a brilliant opportunity for you. Go for it.'

I wasn't angry at all, as it happened. I knew what I'd signed up for by now. A brand new chapter in our lives awaited us, and I felt nothing but excitement.

CHAPTER THREE

SPARRING PARTNERS

OUR FIRST HOME as a married couple was a white 24-foot Hobby trailer, pitched in the yard of Tyson's uncle's house in Lancaster. Uncle Hughie, a renowned boxing trainer, had agreed to coach his nephew as he kicked off his professional career and we thought it'd be sensible to base ourselves at his place, which was situated on a quiet, residential road. We liked the fact there was a large Traveller community in the city, too; we reckoned we'd settle in quite nicely.

Our finances hadn't been able to stretch to a larger static trailer – the type you might see lined up at coastal holiday camps – but this little four-wheeler suited us just fine. The bedroom was at one end, the kitchen was at the other, and in the middle was a small lounge area with bench seats, storage space, a table and a telly. It was a bit of a squeeze – especially for Tyson, who was forever having to crouch down low and mind his head – but we'd both spent much of our childhood living in trailers, so this was nothing new.

Adjacent to our bedroom was a tiny bathroom, which Tyson and I never used, in keeping with the Gypsy way of life. Instead, we'd either use outdoor wash buckets, pop over to Uncle Hughie's for a freshen-up or – if we felt we were imposing on his family – use the facilities at our local leisure centre.

I made our trailer as comfy and as homely as I could. Friends and relatives had bought us lots of soft furnishings as wedding presents – bedding, cushions and tablecloths – and Mam had gifted me a collection of heirlooms that had stayed in our family for generations.

'I'll treasure these,' I said, carefully unpacking the Waterford crystal vases and the Royal Crown Derby crockery. 'And hopefully one day I'll pass them down to *my* kids . . .'

I was quite happy with the idea of becoming a housewife, and putting into practice all the skills I'd learned with Mam through the years. Keeping the trailer spick-and-span, ensuring that Tyson was fed and watered, and – God willing – looking after any children that we might be blessed with in the future, was all fine by me. My plans to follow a career in beauty therapy had been shelved (but not necessarily abandoned) as soon as marriage had appeared on the horizon. If Tyson was to progress as a professional fighter he'd need me to be there for him, practically and emotionally, just like my own mam had supported my dad, and my grannies had supported my grandads. It just felt like the right thing to do. Staying at home was a choice that I'd made myself, of my own free will, and was a choice that I'd never, ever come to regret.

While I kept myself busy in the trailer, Tyson trained extremely hard with Uncle Hughie (my father-in-law John would continue to oversee Tyson's progress, too). A makeshift gym had been constructed in his backyard that, despite being a bit rickety, had everything Tyson needed. Housed in a big brick outbuilding, it comprised a full-size boxing ring on one side, with exercise mats, free weights and boxing bags on the other. Tyson would spend hours working out in 'the shed' with his uncle and other boxers – often from dawn until dusk – and this would create a real racket. Our trailer was only a few metres away, and some evenings I'd have to whack up my DVDs to maximum volume to drown out the boom-boom-boom of glove against bag or the *ooooofs* and *arrrrghs* of a sparring bout.

Over the weeks and months, I learned to live with Tyson's boxing addiction and, by doing so, I discovered the full extent of his training obsession. Everything had to be spot on. He'd get really agitated if his daily routine was delayed or interrupted for any reason so, to keep in his good books, I'd always ensure that his extra-large bowl of breakfast porridge was ready for nine o'clock sharp. I admired Tyson's devotion and ambition – his success would depend on it – but his demanding schedule could sometimes get me down. His one-track mind was always focused on the next training session, so it was often a case of 'Paris, we've got no time to go shopping ... I've got to be back at the gym for five o'clock,' or 'No, we can't have a takeaway on a weeknight, 'cause I'll put on too much weight.'

Ah, just loosen up, will you? I'd think. *A Chinese takeaway isn't going to kill you, for God's sake . . .* But then I'd try to bite my lip, hold my tongue and rein myself in. These sacrifices were being made for a reason, and I had to respect that. But it wasn't easy, and it did create the occasional argument.

As for cooking, I was far from perfect – I was no Nigella, let's say – but I gave it my best shot, managing the food budget, keeping the cupboards well stocked and preparing meals in our little kitchenette. Some days it felt like I was running a mobile cafe, because all I seemed to do was churn out breakfasts, lunches and dinners in order to satisfy Tyson's huge appetite while he was in training mode.

There was no dietician on the scene in those days – that would come further along the line – but Uncle Hughie would sometimes dole out a bit of nutritional advice, asking me to bulk up his boy with massive platefuls of carbs, proteins and vegetables. An average evening meal, therefore, might be hunter's chicken (a fillet wrapped in bacon and sprinkled with grated cheese) served with mashed potato. Drinks-wise, Tyson would guzzle down glasses of his favourite fruit squash – he always cut out caffeine and fizzy pop while he was training – and if he had a snack, it'd either be a piece of fruit or, if he could smuggle it past Hughie, a bar of milk chocolate.

My husband fancied himself as a bit of a chef, as it happened, and would occasionally stage a kitchen takeover.

'Have a night off, for a change,' he'd say with a grin, shooing me away from the oven. 'It's my turn.'

'Do you really have to?' I'd warn as my husband set to his task, clattering the pots and pans. 'You can't cook to save your life.'

He'd never use a recipe book. Instead, he'd just chuck whatever random food he could find at the back of the fridge into a frying pan, throw in any old herb or spice that came to hand and then hope for the best. His speciality was a dish that he christened Chicken à l'Orange, which sounded far more exotic than it actually was. The 'orange' wasn't a delicate hint of citrus, sadly, but was instead a revolting glow-in-the-dark sauce that Tyson concocted by mixing dollops of Hellmann's mayonnaise with a few squirts of Heinz tomato ketchup. Not an orange in sight. To me, it looked totally inedible.

'Mmm, this tastes lovely,' he'd say, wolfing down his creation.

'I'm not actually feeling very hungry at the moment,' I'd say, trying not to hurt his feelings. 'Maybe I'll try some later . . .'

I didn't let him anywhere near our first Christmas dinner – the traditional roast turkey with trimmings – which I somehow managed to rustle up in our tiny oven. I'll forever treasure the memory of us sitting in our cosy trailer, tucking into our festive fare and, for a treat, toasting each other with a glass of Coke.

'Merry Christmas, Paris. Love you . . .'

'Love you too, Tyson . . .'

* * *

If truth be told, our first year of married life was pretty tough. Two strong-willed people living together in a small trailer was never going to be easy, and it took us a while to get used to each other's little ways and habits. I soon realised that cohabiting was a different kettle of fish to courting. You'd learn something new about your partner every day, good or bad. I'd often find myself staring at him and thinking, 'Who are you? Do I actually know you?'

Tyson and I argued constantly back then. We rowed about anything and everything – him breaking a kettle, me losing the trailer keys, him jumping into a bed that I'd just made and arranged cushions on – and it often created a pretty volatile atmosphere. As our temperatures rose, it wasn't unusual for plates to be smashed and glasses to be launched.

Our trailer wasn't the ideal place for a good old fashioned quarrel – there were no lounge doors to slam, or stairs to stomp up – and our effing-and-blinding slanging matches often spilled out onto the street. An hour later, we'd be curled up together on the sofa watching a DVD, having kissed and made up after agreeing that life was too short to argue over a busted Argos appliance. At least living in such a tight space meant that any issues were faced straight away. There was nowhere to hide in a 24-foot trailer.

There'd be times, though, when our non-stop bickering would push me to the limit and I'd find myself packing my bags and flouncing off, vowing never to return.

'I've had enough of all this shit. I'm off to my mam's,' I'd say.

'Oh get gone, then,' he'd reply. 'You've been doing my head in all week. I'm sick of the sight of you.'

The following weekend a sheepish Tyson would roll up to Doncaster, armed with a bunch of flowers, begging me to come back home (which I always did, because I'd miss him terribly). In fact, during our first year of marriage I probably spent the equivalent of six months away from the marital home, to-ing and fro-ing between my husband in Lancashire and my mother in Yorkshire. In those early days, our relationship ran hot and cold like a bath tap.

I was determined to make things work, however, and just saw these quarrels as teething troubles. In the Traveller community (like most others, I guess) once you chose a husband or a wife you were expected to do your utmost to stick with them. Marriage was a serious matter, not a fleeting notion, and you'd only ever consider separation or divorce if there were severe problems in the household, in which case you'd receive all the help and support possible from your wider family to make that break.

I was beginning to learn the effect of Tyson's frequent mood swings, too. I'd been aware of his unpredictable nature when we were dating, but it wasn't until we began living together that I witnessed the full extent of his highs and lows. I'd never known anyone who could be so full of life one week, yet so down in the dumps the next. His gloom would descend without warning – there seemed to be no logic or reason behind it – and he'd veer between spells of deep despair and simmering anger. My attempts to lift his spirits would often fall flat.

'Shall we go for a walk by the river, Tyson?' I'd ask if I noticed he was more withdrawn than usual. 'We can have a nice chat, and get some fresh air.'

'Can't be bothered,' he'd reply, barely able to raise his head to look at me. 'Don't feel like doing anything. Might just go to bed.'

His behaviour made me upset and confused – *surely this isn't what married life is all about?* – and the resentment would grow. Looking back, I was far too young and naive at this point to spot the warning signs, or to recognise any underlying issues. As far as I was concerned, Tyson was acting like a total misery guts, and I had no patience with him.

'What's wrong with you?' I'd demand. 'Why are you sat there with your face inside out? Snap out of it.'

'You don't understand,' he'd respond, shaking his head. 'Just leave me alone, will you?'

That is usually what I'd end up doing. I'd get on with my daily chores and let him stew in his own juices, in the hope that he'd soon regain his mojo. More often than not, a few days later he'd suddenly spring back from Droopy Dog to Papa Smurf, laughing and joking and bouncing around the trailer. Over time, I became used to the ups, downs and loop-the-loops of the Tyson Fury rollercoaster ride. I still loved him to bits, though, moods and all.

One of our cheerier moments took place on a Saturday afternoon in February 2009. Tyson and I were doing the weekly shop at our local Asda, stocking up with the usual essentials, when it was my turn to behave oddly. As we wheeled the trolley down the dairy aisle, I absent-mindedly grabbed a block of Cheddar cheese, unwrapped it from its packaging and bit out a huge chunk.

'What d'you think you're doing, Paris?' hissed Tyson, checking that I hadn't been eyeballed by a security guard. 'We haven't paid for it yet! We'll get done for shoplifting! And you don't even *like* cheese . . .!'

'I don't really know why I did that . . .' I replied, suddenly realising how weird my behaviour must have looked. 'I just felt like eating it, that's all . . .'

A huge grin spread across my husband's face.

'I think I know what all this is about,' he said. 'It's a food craving, isn't it? You're pregnant.'

'Pregnant?' I replied, laughing. 'Don't be so daft! I think I'd know myself if that was the case.'

By the time we reached the store pharmacy, however, Tyson had persuaded me to buy a pregnancy test. I popped into the ladies' loo to do the honours and, sure enough, inside that cubicle just a few minutes later I witnessed that astonishing, life-changing 'blue line' moment. He was right. I *was* pregnant. In the car, as we headed back to Uncle Hughie's, we worked out that I'd probably be due sometime in the autumn.

. It took me a couple of days to recover from the shock – I'd always planned to have a brood of kids, but hadn't expected things to happen so quickly, just months after our wedding.

It took me at least a week to pluck up the courage to tell Mam. I thought she'd be angry with me for a number of reasons: the dust had hardly settled after our marriage, Tyson and I had gone through a few rocky patches, and nineteen was still quite young to be having a baby. In fact, I was so nervous I asked Tyson to gently break the news to her for me. I needn't have worried, though. Mam and the rest of the Mulroys were thrilled to bits, as were my in-laws.

In an instant, Tyson and I grew up. The prospect of us becoming responsible parents later that year made us realise that it was time for the plate-smashing and the slanging matches to stop (as well as the weekend walk-outs). There was a child on the way, and there needed to be some adults in the room.

But, as we began to plan for life with a plus-one, we found ourselves on the move again. There'd been a disagreement between Tyson and Uncle Hughie – one of those 'six of one, half-a-dozen of the other' situations – which prompted Tyson to team up with his dad's other brother, Uncle Peter, who also worked as a boxing trainer. He was based in the village of Warburton Bridge, near Warrington, so we decided to up sticks and tow the trailer down from Lancaster.

By now Tyson's professional career was flourishing, thanks to a string of incredible victories; in April 2009 he knocked out Mathew Ellis at Bethnal Green's famous York Hall and, the following month, he dished out the same punishment to Scott Belshaw at the Watford Colosseum. I attended every fight I could. I loved experiencing the buzz and being part of the action, even though (unlike my cool-headed hubby) I'd be very nervous about the fight itself. On the Wednesday we'd travel over to the venue for the press conference, and on the Thursday Tyson would have a rest day while I shopped in New Look or Topshop for my fight-night outfit. Friday was the all-important weigh-in and Saturday was the main event, after which the two of us would return to our hotel to flop on the bed, watch TV and order a takeaway. Tyson would always be really tired afterwards – fights took so much out of him – and it was nice for us just to be by ourselves, and to hold each other close. The calm after the storm.

What became a very relaxed routine back then would one day become super-regimented, of course. In those days, Team Fury was just his promoter, his trainer . . . and me. From time to time, friends would question my involvement.

'Why on earth d'you go to watch Tyson fight?' I remember a pal once asking me. 'Seeing the man you love getting punched in the face can't be much fun, surely?'

'I have to be there, just to make sure he's all right,' I replied, keen to explain my reasons. 'Let me put it this way. So you're in a pub, and a twenty-two-stone bodybuilder calls your husband out for a fight in the car park. You wouldn't just stay put at the bar with your drink, would you?'

'Er, probably not, no.'

'No. You'd run outside to check that he was OK, because you wouldn't want him to get battered to a pulp. And if he was hurt, you'd want to be there for him, wouldn't you?'

'Yeah, of course I would.'

'Watching Tyson in the ring is not a pleasure, I can assure you. It's a necessity.'

'Fair point, Paris.'

In the middle of a fight my phone would regularly buzz with texts from friends who were watching the bout on TV. They'd feel compelled to tell me I'd been caught on camera, and they liked the new top I was wearing, but would also point out that I looked as miserable as sin. Well, *of course* I had a face like thunder. Witnessing my husband's head being punched repeatedly was never my idea of fun. The only time I was able to crack a smile was out of pure relief, when the final bell rang, signalling the end of the fight and (as was usually the case) a win for the Mancunian in the red corner. To me, boxing wasn't a game. A sport like football or rugby was a game. Boxing was a dangerous business.

There'd be other wives and girlfriends in the crowd, too – there could be a number of fights on the same bill – but I separated them into two distinct camps. You had the partners like me who were there to genuinely support their other halves and who got really involved in the fight, following every punch, round by round. Then you'd have the posing selfie-takers who turned up at the venue just to be seen, and who appeared to pay more attention to their smartphone than the boxing ring.

As Tyson's success grew, so did his fame. Members of the public began to recognise him in the street – in the early days, people would ask for autographs, not selfies – and he started to receive lots of fan mail. The media began to sit up and take notice, too. While his boxing talent was the main focus of their articles, journalists wanted to probe deeper into his Traveller heritage too. They were intrigued by it, asking tons of questions about his culture and its customs. Like me, Tyson was very proud of his Gypsy roots, but he never made a massive deal of it. If anything, he played it down, conscious that he'd been a victim of racial stereotyping when he'd boxed as an amateur.

Tyson's bare-knuckle boxing bloodline was especially fascinating to them. They'd often namecheck his uncle on his dad's side, Bartley Gorman, and his great-uncle on his mam's side, Uriah 'Big Just' Burton, who'd both earned the coveted title of 'King of the Gypsies' in their time. Some sports reporters began to refer to Tyson as the 'Gypsy King', but this didn't always sit well with him. In the early days of his career he much preferred 'Tyson "2-Fast" Fury', a boxing tag he'd thought up as a young kid dreaming of world titles and championship belts. Later on in his career he'd gladly embrace the 'Gypsy King' brand, of course.

TV sports channels were also lining up to request interviews with Tyson and I could see his on-screen personality changing. The shy and introverted young man that I knew began to turn on the bravado. He began to style himself as a tough-talking bad guy, bigging himself up, belittling his opponents and stoking up the pre-fight tension. Tyson had come to realise that professional boxing was as much about entertainment as sport, and that 'celebrity' boxers like

Ricky Hatton and Prince Naseem Hamed commanded more media attention and bigger match fees than their quieter counterparts. This new swagger was winding up a few people – they thought he was arrogant – and he was gaining himself a reputation as a cocky loudmouth. Only those of us who knew Tyson well could see that it was an act, and that he was playing a role. He was just giving the TV companies, the fight promoters and the boxing fans what they wanted, and they lapped up all the soundbites and trash talk.

'Did I do OK?' he'd ask me if I happened to catch him on *Sky Sports News*.

'Yeah, not bad,' I'd say. 'But you do need to stop that habit of talking out of the side of your mouth. You look like some Mafia wise-guy or something. Just speak normally.'

I was Tyson's biggest fan, but I was also his biggest critic.

My husband's rising public profile did have its drawbacks, though, not least the added attention he started to get from other women. He was quite open about it – he'd tell me about the suggestive DMs that arrived in his in-box – but would assure me that everything was ignored or deleted. All this was pretty hard to stomach, especially if I witnessed it with my own eyes. During nights out in Manchester, girls would slide over to the bar and openly flirt with Tyson, even if I was standing by his side. Tyson would be perfectly pleasant – signing autographs, posing for photos – and it was only when he introduced me as his wife that these women would get the message and back off.

In these situations, I'd try hard to stay calm and composed – I'd smile sweetly as they took their pictures – but inside my blood would boil. *What sort of woman hits on a married man?* I'd say to myself. *I'd never dream of doing that . . .*

Tyson would often bear the brunt of my anger in the car as we drove home.

'You *loved* that, didn't you?' I'd yell, as he smiled and shook his head. 'You couldn't get enough of those tramps swarming around you . . .'

'Hey, I can't help it if the ladies love Tyson,' he'd say with a wink, purposely winding me up. 'Who can blame them, eh, Paris? How can anyone resist a good-looker like me?'

'Oh, get over yourself, you big-head . . .'

'Oooooh, touchy . . .'

I'd usually calmed down by the time we got home, my husband having reassured me that he only had eyes for me, and that nothing and no one would ever come between us.

Tyson's early professional successes brought with it some financial rewards, too. In those days he didn't make a fortune, by any means, but he earned enough money for us to comfortably pay our bills and to treat ourselves to a nice meal or a weekend away. Since we didn't have our own accountant, I took it upon myself to manage all of Tyson's paperwork. The business accounting module I'd done at college gave me a basic understanding of finances and I knew the importance of storing receipts and filing tax returns before the correct deadline. Money was never the priority for either of us – until then, we'd lived our lives quite happily without it – but the fact that Tyson was finally making a living felt good, particularly now that there was a baby on the way.

I sailed through the early stages of my pregnancy – no morning sickness or severe fatigue – and was given a due date of 7 October 2009. In the autumn I moved into my mam's house in Doncaster for a while, since Tyson was often away training for an upcoming fight in Ireland and I didn't fancy being alone in the trailer. Around the 36-week mark, I unfortunately suffered a health scare. I was admitted to hospital with a condition called cholestasis – when the flow of bile from your liver is blocked – and was told that it was highly likely that, when the time was right, I'd need an induced delivery. I kept Tyson up to speed by phone – he was very concerned, naturally – but I assured him I was in good hands, I was being well looked after, and he didn't need to dash over.

It was on the eve of his fight, however – while he was in Dublin – that my blood pressure skyrocketed and I had to be rushed to the maternity wing, and put under constant observation. My condition wasn't improving, unfortunately, and so the decision was taken to induce me the following morning.

I rang Tyson to break the news, knowing that it was far too late in the day for his bout to be cancelled. The financial fallout would have been terrible for everyone involved.

His response was classic Tyson.

'Tell those doctors to hold off!' he demanded. 'Tell them to induce you on Sunday instead, so your husband can be there with you . . .'

'It doesn't quite work like that,' I replied. 'Hospitals don't generally revolve around a boxer's fighting schedule.'

Going into labour without Tyson by my side was really upsetting – it was my first child, and I felt I'd been abandoned – but at least I had the support of my mam and her younger sister Romain. Aunt Romain was like a second mother to me, and had made a mad dash from London to Yorkshire to be in the delivery suite. At 7 a.m. on Saturday 26 September Venezuela Lynda Fury safely entered the world, weighing in at eight pounds. And, just a few hours later, Tyson won his fight in Dublin, despite not having slept a wink the night before.

The following morning, The Proudest Dad in the World arrived at my bedside, armed with a pink balloon and a pink teddy bear. Tyson himself chose our daughter's distinctive name – he just thought it sounded beautiful – and I thought it would be nice for her middle name to honour my mam. It brought a tear to my eye to see Tyson cradling the baby for the very first time. Nestled in the crook of his huge, muscly arm, our newborn looked like a tiny china doll.

Motherhood suited me straight away. It seemed to come naturally. I'd always been quite a caring and nurturing person, and felt very comfortable looking after little ones. When I lived at Tilts Farm I often took groups of kids to the local park, or helped them crayon-in their colouring books. My patience levels were pretty high, which no doubt stood me in good stead when my own children arrived.

My daughter happened to be as good as gold, which helped matters. If I could have designed the perfect baby, I'd have probably come up with Venezuela. She fed well, she slept through, and she had such a sunny, giggly nature. I bonded with her instantly – my love for her felt almost over-whelming – and my life suddenly gained more focus and meaning.

With Tyson devoting much of his time to boxing, I knew that Venezuela and I would be spending a lot of time together by ourselves. By then we'd moved temporarily to a rented semi in Manchester close to Jimmy Egan's gym, a renowned boxing academy in Wythenshawe where Tyson was keen to train. I can't say I was massively happy there – it just didn't feel like home, and I found it hard to settle – but I knew I had to be a good wife and mother and make it work. I was keen to become as self-sufficient as possible, and would often refuse help offered by well-intentioned friends and family.

'No, I'll do that,' I said when Mam offered to trim my daughter's tiny fingernails for the first time. 'I need to learn for myself.'

I'd also ask visitors to avoid overly fussing her – no pick-ing her up to soothe her every time she whimpered, for instance – because Venezuela and I were going to be alone a lot and I needed to be the one to calm her, as opposed to relying on others.

Over the weeks and months, I was turning into quite a confident young mother. I was by no means perfect – I often got things wrong, like leaving the baby's bottle at home or forgetting to pack a change of clothing – but, in time, I got to grips with the parenting basics and learned to trust my maternal instincts. I never felt the urge to buy one of those How-To-Raise-Your-Baby books, put it that way.

Tyson was a fantastic dad from Day One. He may have had this reputation as a 'man's man', but Venezuela turned him to mush.

'She's my girl,' he'd say, grinning, as he took her out for a walk around Wythenshawe Park, proudly pushing her in a pink pram.

Once, when Venezuela was just a few months old, Tyson decided to take her to his training gym.

'Put your feet up, Paris, give yourself a break,' he said. 'She'll be fine with me.'

He returned a couple of hours later to tell me that, while sitting in her baby chair, our daughter had been completely mesmerised by the whirrs and rhythms of the exercise bikes and the running machines.

'Ah, that sounds nice,' I said, before a thought struck me. 'Hang on, Tyson . . . where did the baby go when you had a shower?' I assumed the receptionist had kept an eye on her for a few minutes.

'Oh, I took her in with me,' he replied. 'She sat on the floor, splashing away in all the bubbles. She loved it.'

The thought of my precious baby crawling around a men's shower cubicle didn't exactly fill me with joy. It was the first and last time he took her into that shower, that was for sure, although he continued to take her to the gym because she loved it so much.

In December 2010, a couple of months after Venezuela's first birthday, I flew over to Canada to watch Tyson's fight against Zack Page. It would be his first professional bout to take place across the Atlantic – against a very experienced American boxer – and I wanted to witness this major career milestone.

Tyson had been holed up at a US-based training camp for the previous eight weeks. It had been the longest time we'd spent apart since our wedding and I was desperate to see him. I left Venezuela in Doncaster with Mam (who loved having quality time with her granddaughter) and, a few days before the fight, jetted over to Quebec City along with Tyson's promoter, Mick Hennessy, and a boxing coach, John Ingle.

It was the first time I'd flown anywhere without friends or family by my side, so it all felt a little bit strange. Mick and John were nice enough blokes, but I don't recall a lot of conversation taking place between these two middle-aged boxing nuts and a mother-of-one in her early twenties. Maybe I looked a little nervous or awkward in their company, because when we landed at the airport in Canada I was stopped at the departure gates by a pair of stern-looking security guards, who bombarded me with questions. *What was my final destination? Why was I travelling there?* Then they turned their attention to my travel companions.

'Do you know these two men?' they demanded.

'A little bit, but not very well,' I answered, truthfully.

In hindsight, this was probably the wrong thing to say. Before I knew it these officials had pulled me to one side, clearly believing that I was either the victim of some sinister human trafficking plot, or that I was up to no good with a couple of sugar daddies. They continued to quiz me – 'Are you here on your own free will, Mrs Fury?' 'Do you want to tell us something?'– and then searched all my bags and pockets. Eventually I managed to convince them that everything was legit and above board, and they finally waved me through.

It was fabulous to catch up with Tyson in Canada. He was delighted to see me, and during the build-up to the fight I became very much part of his camp, accompanying him to sparring sessions and press conferences. Now that I no longer managed Tyson's financial or business affairs – the entourage had grown to include an accountant – I now played more of a supportive, morale-boosting role. No one cheered louder than me when, following a unanimous decision, Fury claimed victory over Page.

Six months later, Tyson achieved one of his burning ambitions by becoming the British and Commonwealth champion, beating Dereck Chisora at Wembley Arena. It was a brutal fight that left Chisora bloodied and battered, confirmed Tyson's status as an elite boxer, and led to rumours about a future head-to-head with Wladimir Klitschko, the Ukrainian-German world heavyweight champion.

* * *

The spring of 2011 brought very mixed fortunes for the Fury family. On the downside, my father-in-law John was given a jail sentence after being convicted of grievous bodily harm. A dispute with another man had got out of hand, and a brawl had broken out at a local car auction. John had pleaded guilty to the offence, and expressed remorse, but the judge had handed down an eleven-year term. Tyson was devastated to see his dad being locked up. John had been so instrumental in his amateur and professional boxing career – he'd trained him since he was six years old – and he hated the idea of being separated from him.

In much happier news, however, Tyson and I were thrilled to discover that I was pregnant with our second child. Unfortunately, I didn't escape the cholestasis rearing its head again, but I safely gave birth to Prince John James that November, this time with my husband by my side. Tyson and I were so happy to welcome a healthy son into the world, and Venezuela was delighted to have a baby brother. His regal Christian name – chosen by his father, and approved by me – became quite a talking point.

'I'm the king, and he's the prince until he earns his rightful name,' Tyson would explain.

Not long after Prince was born we moved into our first permanent family home, a two-bedroom bungalow in the coastal resort of Morecambe. We'd both become quite fond of the town – we'd visited it a lot when we'd lived in nearby Lancaster – and, although the weather could be pretty wild and windy, we liked the idea of living by the sea. The town's off-the-beaten-track location appealed to us, too. We wanted to raise the kids in as normal an environment as possible, and we felt this might be difficult if we moved over to Cheshire, for example, near where Tyson grew up. Towns like Wilmslow and Alderley Edge were home to many famous footballers and soap stars and, as a result, attracted lots of reporters and paparazzi who'd follow them around all day, every day.

We didn't want our family to live in a goldfish bowl, so were happy to choose Lancashire over Cheshire. It was definitely the right decision. As we settled into Morecambe life, we found we were able to go about our daily business as we pleased without any hassle whatsoever. People became used to seeing the Fury family doing normal, day-to-day stuff – shopping in the local Asda, or wandering along the beach – and they just treated us like ordinary members of the local community. It was a very happy time in our lives; we had our two babies, our new house, and each other, and we couldn't have felt more content.

In January 2012, however, when baby Prince was only six weeks old, our home life was interrupted in dramatic fashion. Tyson had gone to a funeral in Doncaster – one of his uncles had sadly passed away – and me and the kids were going to join him at the wake afterwards. But by the time he came to pick us up from Mam's place, I'd changed my mind.

'The baby looks really, really unwell, Tyson,' I said. 'Something doesn't feel right. I don't think we'll be able to come over.'

Prince had been strangely subdued all day. His breathing had become quite heavy, he'd developed a persistent cough and he seemed really pale and tired.

'You're his mam, Paris, you know best,' Tyson said with concern. 'If your instincts are telling you that something's wrong, perhaps we should get him checked out.'

I didn't need any more prompting to call an ambulance, which luckily arrived straight away, and as the paramedics ran a few checks on Prince I knew I'd done the right thing. They reckoned it was a bad case of infant bronchiolitis and would need further examination at Doncaster Royal Infirmary. I was reassured because I knew the condition was serious but treatable – my nephew had suffered with it in the past – and assumed that, at worst, it'd mean a couple of overnight stays in hospital. I even told Tyson to head back to Morecambe, as I knew he had some important business there.

'You go home, it's fine,' I said. 'I'll stay put with Prince. Venezuela's fine with Mam for the time being. I'll keep you posted, don't worry.'

Prince didn't respond to treatment as expected, however. After four days in hospital his condition began to worsen, so much so that he was unable to breathe independently and had to be sedated and ventilated. The paediatric consultants were so concerned at this sudden deterioration that they decided to transfer him immediately to the special care unit at Sheffield Children's Hospital.

Shell-shocked, I rang Tyson from the ambulance to urge him to drive over as soon as possible. By the time he arrived,

Prince had been admitted into ICU, where he was hooked up to an even bigger ventilator, with lots of plastic tubes and bleeping screens. The sight of our baby son lying on a bed, unconscious and motionless, was just too much to bear. Tyson and I collapsed into each other's arms, sobbing like we'd never sobbed before.

'I'm so scared we're going to lose him,' I said, as my husband hugged me tightly. 'Let's pray he pulls through.'

Further tests confirmed that Prince had developed severe respiratory pneumonia. The medical team told us the next twenty-four hours were critical. He was at the stage where, if his natural defences couldn't fight it off, the doctors could do no more for him. It was in God's hands from that point. Tyson and I hardly left his bedside; we ate, slept and washed at the hospital, as did my mam. The outlook was so grim that many family members came to visit – perhaps to say their goodbyes – although they stayed behind the window to keep any germs at bay.

Much to our relief, the antibiotics gradually began to take effect; Prince's oxygen levels started to increase and he was eventually taken off the ventilator. It was such an incredible feeling to see the colour returning to his cheeks, and to see him smiling and gurgling again.

'We're all so pleased he's on the mend,' said an ICU nurse as we packed Prince's clothes and cuddly toys into his baby bag, in readiness for taking him back home.

'He's a fighter, just like his dad,' said Tyson, smiling.

*   *   *

Prince made a full recovery, thank goodness, and family life slowly returned to normal. Tyson soon got back into the swing of his training programme, which was now taking him overseas. Uncle Peter was still managing Tyson's schedule and had decided that, in between fights, his nephew would benefit from spending time away from the UK. The demands on his time and attention from sponsors, reporters and supporters were threatening to derail his pre-fight preparations, and by setting up training camps around Europe, Tyson would be able to escape the fuss and focus fully on the task in hand. Peter also rated European sparring partners far more highly than their English counterparts.

There was no question of me and the children staying at home while Tyson hopped across the Channel; he hated spending long periods away from the family and always liked me and the kids close by. I was more than happy to pack up our suitcases and join him. I'd always liked to explore new places – roaming around was in my Traveller blood – and I wasn't going to pass up on the chance to see some more of the world.

The Fury Four relished our European travels. By the time Venezuela had started primary school we'd enjoyed spells in France, Italy, Holland, Belgium and Switzerland, often nipping back home to Morecambe for a few weeks in between. Living out of suitcases wasn't a problem for us – we stayed in a succession of hotels, villas and apartments, and once even took a trailer over there – and we made plenty of amazing memories along the way. I remember taking the

kids out into thick, crunchy snow in Holland – the temperatures plummeted to −15 °C that particular winter – and, in
neighbouring Belgium, visiting the lovely city of Antwerp.
During our stay at Lake Lugano – on the Italian–Swiss
border – we enjoyed lots of wonderful walks, visiting pretty
mountainside villages with their timber chalets, ice cream
parlours and coffee shops.

'It's so beautiful here, Tyson,' I'd say, sipping a cappuc-
cino as I admired the lakeside views.

'Bit different to Costa del Lancashire, isn't it?' he'd say
with a grin.

My favourite stopping place had to be Cannes, on the
French Riviera. It felt a little dismal in winter – there wasn't
much going on – but in spring and summer the town burst
into life. While Tyson and Uncle Peter were busy training at
a local gym, Venezuela, Prince and I would stroll along the
marina to have a nosy at all the swanky yachts, or perhaps
have a picnic on the famous La Croisette beach, where many
a movie star had posed and preened during the Cannes Film
Festival.

I even picked up a bit of French during our stay. In other
countries we'd visited – especially Holland – everyone
seemed to speak (and want to speak) English. That wasn't
the case in France, however, and I did my best to get by in
the native language, asking for directions, ordering food
from menus, trying on clothes in shops, that kind of thing.
Tyson and I would have a giggle by using phrasebooks to
chat to each other in very basic French – *tu veux un*

Coca-Cola, mon cheri?' – and promised that, when we returned to the UK, we'd download the Rosetta Stone app to take our language skills up a level. We never did, though; as per usual, life got in the way.

I'd always loved spending time abroad, and I gained so much from our European adventure as well as our holidays to places like Egypt. It reminded me how travel could broaden your mind, create wonderful memories and provide a real insight into how other cultures lived. Our trips abroad gave me a sense of gratitude, too. Spending quality time with Tyson and the kids – particularly in the aftermath of Prince's illness – made me realise exactly how much these special people meant to me. Being alone with my family, without any distractions or interruptions, was like paradise.

CHAPTER FOUR

TRAGEDY & TRIUMPH

BY THE END of 2012, Tyson had won twenty successive professional fights. His undefeated record was a great achievement, and I was so proud of him, but his punishing schedule of bouts was starting to take a toll on our relationship. Fighting three times that year – once in England, and twice in Northern Ireland – meant he'd spent week after week in training camps, mostly away from home. By now Venezuela was attending the local primary school, and Prince was at nursery, so I no longer had the same freedom to hook up with Tyson and his entourage. I never missed the all-important fight night, but – as ever – it was a case of needing to be there for Tyson, rather than relishing the boxing itself.

We spoke regularly on the phone, and sometimes via FaceTime, but inevitably I missed the day-to-day chats, hugs and laughs that you can't get with a remote relationship. Everything was becoming a bit strained, a bit forced. And even though I knew my husband had a job to do, I still felt a little resentful that I was the one stuck in the bungalow, caring for the kids and keeping the place nice. I started to feel quite isolated, and became worried we were growing apart – I could really sense the distance widening between us – and I think Tyson felt the same.

In the spring of 2013, Tyson flew over to New York City to prepare for his upcoming fight against Steve Cunningham. I began to make arrangements to join up with him in April, just prior to the bout. The kids were still a bit too young to travel such a distance, I reckoned, so my mam and my best friend Shannon agreed to look after them for a few days. They were a godsend to me – they often helped out with childcare – and I couldn't thank them enough.

Shortly before I left I received a call from Tyson.

'I've been having a think, Paris, and I've got an idea.'

'Go on . . .'

'When you come over to New York we should renew our wedding vows.'

'Seriously?'

'Yeah, I'm serious. I know it's been tough for you lately, and I just think it would be a nice thing for us to do. A fresh start. I've found a church in Manhattan that looks perfect. What d'you reckon?'

'I'd love that, Tyson. I really would.'

I shed a little tear when he ended the call. Tyson could be a complete arse sometimes – he knew it, and I knew it – but, when he was in the right mood, he could also be very thoughtful and romantic, and here he was again showing just how much he cared. The longer our marriage went on, the more I realised it was all or nothing with my husband.

With Mam on my Christening Day in 1990. I'll be forever grateful for having such a kind and caring person as my mother.

My first day at Arksey Primary School, near Doncaster, in 1994.

The Mulroy children looking smart in our Sunday best. From left to right: me, Montana, Jimmy and Romain, 1993.

With my friend Maria at the wedding reception in Nottingham in 2005 where I first met Tyson.

At home with Tyson on my 16th birthday. We weren't yet dating, but we both sensed a spark between us.

After we officially became a couple in December 2005.

Practising my beauty therapy treatments on Tyson while I was studying for my NVQ in 2006.

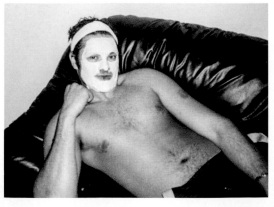

Loved up at the Appleby Horse Fair in Cumbria in 2007, a major event in the Travellers' social calendar.

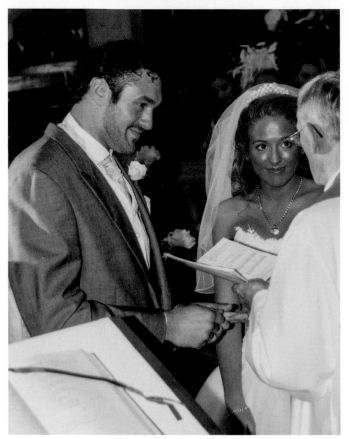

Exchanging our marriage vows at St Peter-in-Chains Roman Catholic Church in Doncaster, on Friday 21st November 2008.

With my beautiful bridesmaids at my wedding reception in South Yorkshire, including my sisters Montana (second left) and Romain (far right).

A proud mam and dad cradling their baby daughter, Venezuela Lynda, born in September 2009.

Four generations together: Mam, baby Venezuela, me and Granny Mary.

Outside our rented accommodation with Venezuela in Manchester, winter 2010.

Tyson with the English championship belt in 2010 as his career went from strength to strength.

One of our first trips after Prince John James was born in November 2011, this one to Egypt.

Renewing our wedding vows in New York City in spring 2013.

My mam with 'her girls' – Romain, Montana and me – at Montana's wedding in 2015.

Tyson making his memorable entrance to the Fury v Klitschko press conference in September 2015 in his too tight Batman costume.

A tearful reunion in the ring with my husband following his stunning victory over Klitschko in Düsseldorf in November 2015.

After the victory, Tyson paying tribute to his beloved late uncle Hughie with his image on his t-shirt. Behind are Shane (left), Johnboy (right) and cousin Hughie (middle).

Attending the difficult night of the 2015 BBC Sports Personality of the Year Awards in Belfast.

An outing to Morecambe's Midland Hotel with our newborn son, Prince Tyson Luke, in July 2016. The strain of Tyson's mental health on our marriage was beginning to show.

He was a creature of extremes. Some days he'd ignore me for hours, moping about in a mood and leaving me feeling unloved, but other days he'd treat me like a queen, taking me into Lancaster for a fancy meal and making me feel special. If he wasn't giving me the cold shoulder, he'd be kissing my feet. I'd only find out later that this yo-yo behaviour bore all the hallmarks of someone with a bipolar disorder but of course I had no idea at the time. With Tyson, I just learned to expect the unexpected.

The fight against Cunningham took place at Madison Square Garden and proved to be an emotional rollercoaster. Although Tyson won easily in the end, in round two he was knocked to the floor for only the second time in his professional career (the first having been at the hands of Neven Pajkić, five months earlier). Watching my husband hit the deck was a shocking new experience for me – I'd become used to feeling sorry for the guy in the other corner – and I found it very, very scary.

The knockdown was over in seconds but, as I watched from my ringside seat, it seemed to happen in slow-motion. I remember feeling totally helpless as Cunningham's upper-cut connected with Tyson's jaw and caused him to tumble to the floor. I can only liken it to that moment when your toddler is running around a park and you see they're going to trip over a fallen log or a jutting brick. You hear yourself yelling at them from afar, you find yourself sprinting towards them like Usain Bolt, but you know you're too late – there's nothing you can do, and within moments they're going to fall and badly hurt themselves. Just yards away from the boxing ring, I felt that same sense of hopeless panic.

While I watched the referee giving Tyson the count ('six . . . seven . . . eight . . .') a realisation hit me like a ton of bricks: my husband was not invincible.

Wow. You've just been hurt, I kept repeating to myself, as Tyson got back to his feet. *Somebody's actually hurt you.*

Much to my relief Tyson responded brilliantly, wearing Cunningham down with his superior strength and power and eventually knocking him out in the seventh round. But I had no appetite for celebrating, because I was still reeling from seeing him spreadeagled on the canvas. I wasn't the only family member to be left shell-shocked. Tyson's brothers Shane and Hughie, who'd also travelled to New York and had been following his fights for longer than me, said it was the first time they'd seen him in that situation. Tyson, however, was remarkably calm when we met up with him in the dressing room afterwards. He simply brushed off the knockdown. As far as he was concerned, he'd recovered and won the fight, and had maintained his unbeaten record. Both boxes had been ticked, and that was what mattered most.

'You can't go swimming and not get wet, Paris,' he said as he gave me a sweaty hug. Getting hurt was only to be expected in boxing. It really didn't faze him.

In fact, Tyson had been so relaxed after the final bell that he'd grabbed a microphone and treated the crowd to a rendition of a country song called 'Keep It Between the Lines'. He'd always loved to belt out a tune – he did it all the time at home and in the car – and his boxing ring sing-songs were now becoming part of his 'show'.

The following afternoon, Tyson and I renewed our wedding vows at a Roman Catholic church in downtown Manhattan. It was a simple ceremony, nothing formal. I was dressed just in a pair of black leggings and a plain white blouse, and Tyson wore a casual suit. We were keen for the occasion to be as low-key as possible, so the only others present were Shane, Hughie and the priest.

The ceremony was short but meaningful. We listened to a lovely Bible reading, we exchanged special rings we'd bought that morning, and we recited our respective vows to each other. It all felt quite emotional, to be honest, and both Tyson and I had lumps in our throats. That sense of drifting away from each other had been awful – we'd lost a certain closeness and intimacy – but as we stood at the altar, holding hands, we felt like husband and wife again.

Back home in Morecambe, Tyson entered into discussions with his manager, Mick Hennessy, about his next career move. Following his gutsy victory against Steve Cunningham, he was keen to step things up a gear with a money-spinning bout against a big-name opponent. Since becoming professional, Tyson's fee for each fight – the so-called 'purse' – had been sizeable but, even though we weren't complaining, his earnings were by no means in the million-dollar megabucks league. That was usually reserved for the 'box office' stars, like the American Floyd Mayweather and the Ukrainian Klitschko brothers, Vitali and Wladimir. Fame and fortune had never been Tyson's prime motivation – titles meant more to him than wealth – but the idea of setting up our family for life, in a financial sense, had always been a goal of his. A boxing career could be short – and risky – and, from Tyson's perspective, it was a case of making hay while the sun shone, at a time when he believed he could beat anyone. I understood where he was coming from. Tyson wasn't particularly bothered about becoming a 'celebrity' – both he and I were quite happy to keep our feet on the ground in Morecambe, far away from the limelight – but if a high-profile boxing match could secure our family's future, then he'd be the first to sign on the dotted line.

Tyson's dream looked like it might become a reality in the summer of 2013 when former world heavyweight champion and fellow Brit, David Haye – the so-called 'Hayemaker' – announced he was willing to take on Tyson in his next fight. This was incredible news. This high-profile showdown would most likely be broadcast on the pay-per-view Sky Box Office channel, which would make it the biggest and most lucrative bout of Tyson's career. A date was set for Saturday 28 September and – much to Team Fury's delight – the venue was confirmed as the Manchester Arena. For years, Tyson had longed to fight in his home town, in front of his own supporters, and he was beyond excited. I felt genuinely thrilled for him. I hadn't seen him so buzzing in ages.

He immediately set up an intensive training camp near Manchester, digging deep into his own pockets to secure the best team, the best sparring partners, the best workout gym and the best accommodation. He'd be earning millions from this fight, so he felt confident it was money he'd eventually get back.

With Team Fury HQ just an hour's drive away from Morecambe, the children and I were able to visit Tyson fairly regularly. While his spare time was limited – he was so focused on the upcoming fight – we managed to find windows of opportunity. Every Thursday he and I would have a date night, meeting halfway for a bite to eat or to watch a movie, and each weekend I'd bring the kids over to Manchester so we could all have Sunday lunch together.

I remember being in Tyson's hotel room – only a week before the big fight – when his cousin, also called Hughie, suddenly burst in and told us to switch on Sky Sports News.

'What's going on?' asked Tyson.

'Just wait and see,' Hughie replied. 'You're not going to be happy.'

We watched, open-mouthed, as the presenter announced that Haye had cancelled the fight, saying he'd badly cut his eye during a sparring session and releasing a photo of the wound to the media. Tyson was dumbstruck. He simply couldn't believe what was happening. He sat on the end of the bed, shaking his head in disbelief, as I offered him a comforting hug. I was gutted, too. This fight meant the world to him, and he'd trained so hard for it.

The date for Haye v Fury was quickly rearranged – it would now take place on Saturday 8 February, at the same venue – and Tyson set up yet another training camp, this time in Bolton. But within weeks Haye had cancelled that fight, too, having now suffered a shoulder injury. Tyson took it all very badly. Not only was his dream fight in tatters – it was now unlikely it would ever happen, due to Haye's injuries – our bank account had also been massively dented. Tyson had invested a huge amount of his own money in both training camps and, while we weren't expecting bailiffs at our door, we found ourselves having to keep to a much tighter budget, with any dreams of financial security now on hold. Two more fights would take place later that year – against Joey Abell and Dereck Chisora, both in London – but neither had the same profile or appeal as a head-to-head with Haye.

In the spring of 2014, and not for the first time in our marriage, I saw my husband's behaviour dip; looking back, it was probably his first serious bout of depression. As the disappointment of the Manchester non-event sank in, his mood darkened and he seemed to lose all his focus and motivation. Tyson also developed a drinking habit, which was totally out of character. Like me, he'd never been interested in alcohol, only very occasionally having a small lager at a party just to blend in with the crowd. In fact, he used to go out of his way to avoid boozed-up people because they'd often drunkenly challenge him to a fight, for a laugh.

'Only slinks drink,' he'd say, 'slink' being a Traveller term for 'loser'.

Since then something had clearly changed, and a couple of times a week he'd return home from the local pub, a bit worse for wear, telling me he was done with boxing.

'I've had enough, Paris. I'm quitting,' he'd say, slurring his words.

'Don't be so daft,' I'd say. 'There's plenty of life left in you yet. Go and get yourself a good sleep. You might feel differently in the morning.'

As I'd done back in our Lancaster trailer days, I tried – and usually failed – to lighten his mood and chivvy him along. There was only so much I could do, and more often than not I'd end up leaving him to his own devices, silently hoping and praying that the black cloud would pass. By not making a fuss about Tyson's mood swings, I was also trying to protect the children. They were no longer babies – by then Venezuela was four, and Prince was two – and I didn't want them to hear any raised voices or sense any bad vibes. And there was one more important reason for trying to keep our family life as stress-free as possible: I was pregnant again.

Tyson and I had always intended to carry on the great Traveller tradition and have a big family: three children at the very least, we'd say to each other, maybe even ten if we were lucky. We'd already made a pretty good start, to be fair. Prince had arrived fairly quickly after Venezuela, in November 2012, and once he'd celebrated his first birthday we'd started to think about adding to our brood. Our plans ended up being delayed, because I had to undergo some surgery – let's call it a 'woman's problem' – and was advised to give myself a few months to recover. It took me a good year after that to conceive, but in the summer of 2014 I was delighted to discover I was expecting.

The baby news gave Tyson a welcome boost – he was overjoyed – and also acted as a distraction from his emotional struggles. I often found myself steering our conversation towards planning for the new arrival, and we'd discuss the idea of relocating to a bigger house in Morecambe (space was going to be an issue in our two-bedroom bungalow) or whether we'd be shopping for girls' things or boys' things in baby shops.

When I was five months pregnant, however, I suffered some complications and Tyson had to rush me into hospital. Following some tests and scans, we received the devastating news that the baby's heart had stopped beating. There was nothing the medical team could do. A midwife then gently broke the news to me that, although the baby was no longer alive, its advanced development meant I had no other option but to proceed with a delivery.

Never in my life had I felt so scared and upset. I rang Mam in tears, asking her to drive over to the hospital – you never stop needing your mother, no matter how old you are – and she and Tyson were by my side to give me all the love and care I needed to get through this nightmare. All I'll say is I'd hate any other woman to experience in their lifetime what I had to endure that day. It was crushing.

Tyson was distraught, but still managed to be my rock throughout, squeezing my hand, stroking my forehead, telling me over and over again how much he and the kids loved me. But even as he sank deeper into his own despair, he summoned the strength to do something that, to this day, still amazes me. Tyson was insistent that the baby should be laid to rest on our terms and, having discussed the situation with the doctors, he took its little body away. He found a wooden box and buried the baby in a secluded spot in his father's garden, before saying a few prayers, shedding a few tears, and laying down a stone to mark the resting place.

Initially I'd wanted to attend this private burial – I'd been discharged from hospital a few hours earlier – but Mam persuaded me to stay away, worried it would be far too traumatic for me, given the fragile state I was in, both physically and emotionally. I felt so sad not to be there but now, in hindsight, I think it was a sensible decision for me.

If the trauma of losing a baby wasn't enough, more tragedy was to hit the Fury family. Tyson's Uncle Hughie had suffered a terrible accident, just as I was going through my ordeal. He'd broken his leg while trying to move a caravan and had been rushed to A&E at the same hospital I was in. At one point Tyson found himself frantically dashing from one ward to another. My heart went out to him for what he must have been going through, seeing us both suffering. But worse was to follow for Hughie. Shortly afterwards he was struck down with a blood clot, which travelled up to his lung and triggered a cardiac arrest. He slipped into a coma. For almost three months the family kept a constant vigil by his bedside.

While this drama was unfolding Tyson was also pulling out of a fight against Belarusian boxer Alexander Ustinov. His head was all over the place and he was in no fit state to compete. Stepping into the ring, weighed down with worries, would have put his own safety at risk. Elite boxing demanded one hundred per cent focus – always a speciality of Tyson's – and just one brief lapse in concentration might have been harmful, even fatal. It would have been a reckless decision to continue with the fight, and the whole family felt very relieved when it was cancelled.

'Thank God for that, Tyson,' said Shane. 'I can't believe you were even considering it in the first place. You need to be kind to yourself.'

Hughie never woke up from his coma and died three months later in October 2014. Tyson was utterly heart-broken. His uncle had almost been like a second father to him while his own was in prison and, despite having parted with him as his trainer, they'd remained very close. Tyson would always appreciate the contribution that Hughie had made to his boxing career and, as a couple, we'd be forever grateful to him for introducing us to Lancashire life. Had we not pitched up next to Hughie's house in the early days of our marriage, we'd have never ended up settling in Morecambe.

After the stillbirth, I felt the need to return to my normal routine. I knew that getting back into the swing of things, and occupying myself with the daily rituals of family life, would give me some comfort. Focusing on everyday tasks, like doing the weekly shop, cooking Tyson his favourite meals and reading the kids their bedtime stories, would massively help my recovery.

I chose not to talk to anyone about my miscarriage. I felt there wasn't much more I could say; I'd lost a baby, and no words could change that. And while Tyson and I had cried buckets of tears in the hospital, and had clung to each other like a pair of koala bears, in the aftermath we felt there was no point in raking everything up and reliving the nightmare. We never spoke much about the baby. It had happened, and it had been horrendous, but we both agreed to try to move forward, and stay strong for the sake of the family. We'd cherish the beautiful children we already had, and would try to look to the future rather than dwelling on the past.

My friends and family were really kind and thoughtful – they rang up to tell me how sorry they were, and to check I was OK – but, once I started asking them about their kids' birthdays or their holiday plans, they soon realised that I preferred not to linger over my sad experience. Had I wanted to talk things through, each member of this lovely support network would have listened to me all day long. It was my decision not to, though, and they respected that. It may not have been everyone's way of facing it – I appreciate that other women suffering a similar loss might have preferred to discuss their feelings – but it was right for me. Not talking about my loss didn't mean I felt any less devastated. Everybody grieves differently, of course. There isn't a right or wrong way to get over the death of a loved one. It is an intensely personal thing. I agree with whoever said that we are 'the experts of our own lives'. Only you know how you feel, and this approach was right for me.

As time went on, however – and as Prince approached his fourth birthday – I began to yearn for another child. It had all gone worryingly quiet on that front, and I'd started to convince myself something was wrong, and that I'd never conceive again. A few people told me not to panic, and to just let nature take its course ('It's all in your head, Paris . . .' they said) but it reached the stage when I could hardly think about anything else. My biological clock was ticking louder than ever and, as each month passed, I became more and more disheartened. Sometimes I'd get annoyed at myself for being so selfish – *for God's sake, woman, be thankful you've been blessed with a healthy son and daughter* – but I couldn't get over the fact that I'd always imagined having loads of children.

I was desperate to understand the problem – and to solve it if there was one – and after discussing it with Tyson, we booked ourselves into an NHS fertility clinic in Lancaster to get checked out. The staff at the clinic were lovely, and made us feel very much at ease. It took a few hours for all the procedures and assessments to take place – both Tyson and I underwent tests – and we returned to the clinic a fortnight later to get the results. It had been a very anxious wait for both of us.

'You'll be pleased to hear your tests have come back clear, and we couldn't find any significant issues with either of you,' said the consultant, as he studied the records on his computer screen. 'You don't need any fertility treatment, Mrs Fury, so there's no reason why you shouldn't be able to conceive naturally.'

Great, so it IS all in my head . . . I remember thinking to myself.

'But the problem remains that you're still not having any luck getting pregnant,' he continued, 'and seeing as we can't find any issues, and seeing as you don't require fertility treatment, all I can suggest is a course of IVF.'

I immediately burst into tears. At that moment, I felt my world had caved in. So they couldn't *find* a problem, but I still *had* a problem. It wasn't the news I wanted to hear.

After a quiet journey back home to Morecambe, Tyson and I had a heart-to-heart. I was ready and willing to kick-start the IVF process – I just couldn't wait any longer – but Tyson reckoned we should hang fire for a while.

'Whatever will be, will be,' he said. 'If we're meant to have more children, God will give us more children. I know it's hard for you, but please give it more time.'

'But how much longer do I have to wait, Tyson?' I replied. 'One year? Two years? Or even five years? I'll be pushing thirty by then.'

We finally reached a compromise. If I didn't conceive within twelve months, I'd go ahead with the IVF treatment.

And, with that decision done and dusted, I stopped obsessing, and began to get on with my life.

After a terrible 2014, the following year started more positively for the Fury family. Having served four years of his sentence, John was released from prison and returned home to Manchester. Tyson was delighted to have his father back in his life, both personally and professionally. His mood was still more down than up, and he was still mourning the loss of the baby and his uncle, but John's presence in the Bolton gym seemed to lift his spirits a little. Together with Uncle Peter, Team Fury began to prepare for the upcoming fight against Romanian-German Christian Hammer. This was a vital bout for Tyson. Victory would almost certainly give him a crack at the world heavyweight title – the fight he'd always dreamed of – namely a showdown against the biggest star in boxing, Wladimir Klitschko.

I was among the crowd at London's O2 Arena on Saturday 28 February to watch Tyson completely overpower Hammer. The opposite corner threw in the towel after eight rounds, their man having been knocked down in the fifth. It should have been a real time of joy, but Tyson wasn't his usual self. The showman had all but disappeared and he hardly celebrated in the ring afterwards; he did the opposite, in fact, and just stared downcast at the floor. I was probably the only person in that venue who knew exactly what was going on behind the scenes.

A few weeks later, the date was set for Klitschko v Fury – it would take place in Düsseldorf, Germany (the opponent's adopted homeland) on Saturday 24 October – and the count-down to the biggest fight in Tyson's life began. Again, what should have been a happy time was anything but. His mood was really low, and his motivation seemed to nosedive.

'I can't be bothered with it all, Paris,' he said, during one of his bleaker moments, telling me once again that he hated competing and was finished with boxing.

'Come on, Tyson, you know you can do it,' I said, although I doubted my positive words were hitting home. I was slowly beginning to realise there was only one person who could change his mindset: Tyson himself. But I'd no idea what it would take for that to happen.

The fight preparations continued regardless – I think it was a case of 'the show must go on' – and intensive training camps (or 'fat camps', as Tyson called them) were set up in Liverpool and Cannes. Having tipped the scales at twenty-five stone, Tyson needed to lose at least six of them to reach his fighting weight, and was put on a super-strict protein shake diet. From my perspective, I didn't really care how big he was – I adored my husband, whatever his weight – but I knew he had to hit peak condition if he was to beat Klitschko, who'd remained undefeated in eleven years and whose strength had earned him the nickname 'Dr Steelhammer'.

The pre-fight press conference took place at the Hilton London Syon Park hotel on Wednesday 23 September and, thanks to Tyson, it hit all the sports headlines. He'd been in one of his 'hyper' moods the day before – he was rarely on an even keel back then – and, as we'd watched TV in our hotel room, he'd come up with a crazy plan.

'I'm going to liven things up a bit tomorrow, and really get into Klitschko's head,' he said. 'I'm going to turn up dressed as Batman.'

'Don't be silly, you can't do that,' I said, laughing.

But he was deadly serious. He called up a friend in London, who managed to get hold of a Batman suit at lightning speed from a local fancy dress shop and then dropped it off at our hotel.

There was a slight problem, though. The costume clearly hadn't been designed for an XXXL professional boxer. Watching Tyson trying to squeeze himself into it is one of the funniest things I've seen in my life. I was howling with laughter as he tried (and failed) to zip it up.

'Tyson, your bum and your back are hanging out,' I said between giggles. 'There's no way you can wear that.'

'Course I can,' he said with a grin, brandishing Batman's long black cape. 'This'll cover everything.'

The following day I watched from the audience as Tyson burst into the press conference wearing his superhero costume, complete with black face mask. The whole room fell about laughing as the *Batman* theme tune blared out – even the serious-minded Klitschko cracked a smile – and the press photographers had a field day, clicking away to get their best shot of this bizarre sight. They probably assumed Tyson had been planning this crazy PR stunt for weeks, and that it had all been well-rehearsed. But nothing was further from the truth. Like so many things in my husband's life, it had all been done on a whim. I was so pleased to see the showman return, though.

Tyson was in full stride now and proceeded to take over the press conference. Following a quick costume change (the Batman suit was replaced with a smart, tailored check suit) he grabbed the microphone and encouraged various reporters to ask him questions. At one stage – much to my surprise – he pointed the mic at me.

'The beautiful woman in the front row with the blond hair . . . what's your question?' he said, with a wink and a smile. That was me put on the spot. I just fired off the first question that came into my head.

'How much d'you love me?' I asked.

'The whole wide world,' he replied.

As it happened, the big fight ended up being postponed by a month, to Saturday 28 November – Klitschko needed extra time to recover from a calf injury – but the media attention continued. Every sports fan in the country seemed to be talking about it. Most of the boxing press had Tyson down as the underdog – they were entitled to their opinion, of course, but it wound me up watching TV pundits saying that, while it was great to see a British fighter challenging at this level, he didn't have a chance of beating Klitschko.

'For goodness sake!' I'd yell at the telly. 'Have some faith in him, why don't you!'

In early November, sections of the media had also jumped on some comments Tyson had made in an interview – things he really shouldn't have said – and which led to him hogging the headlines for all the wrong reasons. While there was quite a lot of anti-Fury feeling going around, he could still rely on the support of his huge, loyal fan base.

A week or so before the fight, I went on my sister Montana's hen night in Leeds. She was due to marry her boyfriend Billy the following month, with Romain and me as her bridesmaids. It was nice to have a break from all the boxing shenanigans, and it was great to get together with so many friends, aunts and cousins. I even allowed myself a small glass of champagne as we all toasted the bride-to-be.

The following day, however, I woke up feeling sickly and lethargic. I assumed it was a mild hangover since my body wasn't used to alcohol, even tiny amounts. I didn't feel any better the next day, either, so I rang Montana to have a moan.

'Paris, have you thought about doing a pregnancy test?' she asked.

'Nope, no way, there's no need for that,' I said. With every-thing going on fight-wise, and with the kids keeping me busy at home, I'd had no time to fixate upon babies. In any case, I'd come to the conclusion I could no longer conceive naturally.

Following some sisterly persuasion, I went out and bought a test and watched, stunned, as that telltale blue line slowly appeared.

Wow, I'm pregnant. After all this time, I'm actually pregnant . . .

I was gobsmacked. I could only assume that, by taking the pressure off myself, my stress levels had reduced, my body had relaxed and my hormones had fired into action.

After a great deal of thought, I decided not to tell Tyson straight away. There was just a week to go until the big bout – Team Fury had already decamped to Düsseldorf – and I was afraid this baby news (amazing though it was) would throw him off track.

I travelled to Germany five days before the fight, leaving Venezuela and Prince in the capable hands of my mam in Morecambe. Just to be on the safe side, and not wanting to take any risks, I decided against flying. Our good friends Dave and Cathy Reay had already made plans to drive over – they were taking some extra equipment as a favour to Tyson – and they kindly let me jump in with them. We'd known the Reays for years. Dave had been a good friend of Uncle Hughie's, and he and Tyson had bonded over their love of off-road cars. I'd also become very close with his wife Cathy, and my best friend Shannon was their daughter (I had been proud to be Shannon's 'best woman' at her wedding). All three were part of a tight-knit group of lovely, long-standing friends who Tyson and I could trust with our lives.

My journey to Düsseldorf with the Reays took much longer than expected. The terrible terrorist attacks in Paris had taken place ten days previously; security was understandably high everywhere and we had to pass through numerous checkpoints along the route.

After six weeks apart, Tyson and I were thrilled to see each other – there were lots of hugs and kisses – and, with my little secret at the forefront of my mind, I could hardly wipe the smile off my face. I was relieved to see him in pretty good shape, physically and emotionally; his training had gone well, he'd hit his target weight, and his confidence was high. It was so great to see him back on top form. Tyson liked having goals in his life, and there was no bigger target than this. Having his father in his entourage for the first time in four years had also given him a big boost.

For the first few days I managed to keep my mouth shut about the pregnancy, but on the eve of the fight, while we were in our hotel room, I couldn't hold on any longer. Tyson's relaxed state of mind had convinced me he'd be able to handle things well. I was a bit of a tease when it came to the big reveal, though.

'If you heard some good news before a fight, Tyson, would it affect you?'

'I don't think so. Nothing would get in the way of this fight. But I suppose it would depend what the good news was.'

My Cheshire cat smile must have given the game away, because Tyson's eyes lit up.

'You're pregnant, aren't you?' he said.

I nodded my head, and we both fell into each other's arms.

The following morning, Tyson and I woke up and ordered a healthy breakfast of porridge and banana (I always ate the same food as him on fight day; it'd be unfair of me to sit there with a fry-up or a bacon sandwich). As I flicked through the sports TV channels it was clear to see that Klitschko v Fury was the biggest story in town – 'the richest prize in boxing', they were calling it – although I can't say that pound signs were at the forefront of my mind. Above all, I just wanted Tyson to come through the fight unscathed. He'd fought some decent boxers in the past, but none of them had the punching power of Klitschko.

'So how are you feeling, then?' I asked him, as I sipped my orange juice.

'Good,' he said, smiling, with a calm nod of the head. 'Feeling good.'

Later that day Tyson and I made our way to the Esprit Arena – we always travelled to the fight together – and after spending a couple of hours with him in the dressing room, I took my ringside seat next to his elder brother, John Boy. I always liked to dress up for fight night, and this particular outfit – like many of my favourite get-ups – was a mix 'n' match of designer and high street. I wore a short black dress from TK Maxx that had cost me about fifteen quid, a black Moschino jacket with gold sequin dollar signs that came with a hefty price tag, and a pair of River Island stilettos.

The atmosphere in the arena was electric – there was a real buzz of expectation among the 55,000 capacity crowd – but for me there was just that familiar mixture of pre-fight dread and anxiety. This time it felt worse than ever, and I felt sick to my stomach. The entertainment programme was in full swing, too, with Rod Stewart topping the bill. No disrespect to Rod, but I was far too nervous to focus on his singing. Not that I'd have been able to see his performance anyway. Two very tall, slim women in minidresses – models, I assumed – had decided to block my view while gyrating to the music. I got the impression that these girls were there for a party, not for the boxing, and the more they danced around, the more they began to bother me. My anxiety levels were sky-high, granted – with some pregnancy hormones thrown in for good measure – and their twirling and twerking really got my back up. It just seemed inappropriate in the circumstances. In twenty minutes' time my husband would be undertaking the most important fight of his life. He'd be going out of the trenches. There was a chance he could get badly hurt. His life might even be in danger. This felt like a war, not a disco, and I couldn't hold back.

'Could you move, please?' I asked the girls through gritted teeth. 'You're in the way.'

Unable to hear me in the din, they just shrugged their shoulders and carried on dancing. As the red mist started to rise, I found myself nudging Tyson's brother.

'John, I've never hurt anyone in my life, but I've got this crazy urge to boot these girls up their skinny, miniskirted arses.'

He chuckled. 'Please don't do that, Paris. Firstly, there are cameras about. Secondly, there's only one Fury that should be fighting tonight.'

The disco divas eventually wiggled their way back to their seats, and the stage was set for Tyson's big entrance. Dressed in a green and gold robe, he shadow-boxed into the arena to the soundtrack of one of his favourite songs, Randy Travis's 'I'm Gonna Have a Little Talk with Jesus'. I felt so proud of him; he'd spent his whole life waiting for a moment like this. After climbing into the ring he took off his robe, revealing a pair of green and gold shorts with 'Venezuela' emblazoned on the back and 'Prince' on the front. On his white T-shirt was an image of Uncle Hughie, with the words 'God Is All Things Most High. RIP.' I'd known beforehand that Tyson was going to wear this, but it still felt very emotional to see it on the night.

I can't say I paid much attention to Klitschko's subsequent arrival, though. My focus was solely on Tyson.

'He looks really calm, doesn't he?' I said to John Boy.

'Calmer than anyone else in here,' he said, smiling, as the atmosphere reached fever pitch.

From that point on my memories are really hazy. When the fight began I felt weirdly detached, like it was some out-of-body experience. I can vividly remember my thought processes, though, as the minutes ticked by. I went from *'Please don't get hurt, Tyson . . .'* at the start to *'Hey, he's doing OK, isn't he?'* as he seemed to settle into the bout. As he progressed through each round I started to feel more confident, going from *'Is it me, or is he taking control here?'* to *'OH MY GOD, TYSON'S WINNING THIS!!!'* When the final bell rang after the twelfth round, half of me felt relieved and the other half excited. Relieved that he'd emerged from the fight without getting hurt (there wasn't a mark on his face, unlike

Klitschko) and excited that the bold promise he'd made to me on a Doncaster hillside, all those years ago, might just have come true.

The final verdict seemed to take an eternity, long enough to scare me that he'd fall victim to some kind of injustice ('I hope he doesn't get robbed,' I said to John Boy). I needn't have worried. Following a unanimous decision, my husband was officially crowned the new heavyweight boxing champion of the world. Against all the odds, he'd bossed the biggest fight of his life and beaten the great Wladimir Klitschko on his home turf. I couldn't stop the tears from flowing as Tyson jumped around the ring in glee, before being mobbed by his entourage.

I hadn't intended to climb into the ring myself, mainly because my TK Maxx dress was on the short side and I didn't want to have a wardrobe malfunction on live television. But having tried in vain to get Tyson's attention – and seeing half his family clambering in to celebrate with him – I thought *sod it* and slid between the ropes, trying to keep any leg-flashing to a minimum. I managed to give Tyson a brief hug, and to say a quick 'I love you', before he took the microphone to deliver his post-fight speech.

There was hardly a dry eye in the Team Fury camp as he thanked Jesus Christ for inspiring him to glory, acknowledged his Uncle Peter for all his help and guidance, and dedicated the fight to the memory of Uncle Hughie. Then, after paying tribute to his opponent, Tyson rounded things off in his own special way.

'I promised everybody I'd sing a song after this fight, so this is to my UK fans, my Irish fans, my American fans, and my new German fans,' he said. 'But most of all, this is dedicated to my wife.'

As I stood in the ring, my eyes brimming with tears, he serenaded me with a rendition of Aerosmith's 'Don't Want to Miss a Thing'. It was totally off the cuff – he'd not planned it in advance – but it was such a sweet thing to do; sometimes I hated his crazy, unpredictable nature, but sometimes I loved it, too. There may have been thousands of people in the stadium that night, and millions of viewers watching worldwide, but for that brief moment in time it felt like it was just the two of us standing there.

Back at our hotel, hundreds of boxing fans were celebrating Tyson's victory (the whole downstairs foyer was jam-packed) but the pair of us managed to sneak past them unnoticed. Tyson was incredibly flattered to see all this support for him but, after the exertions of the fight (and a very long press conference) he needed some rest. He left his newly acquired title belts with his team, though, so supporters could have their photographs taken with them.

We headed back home to England the following day with Dave and Cathy, driving from Düsseldorf to Rotterdam before catching an overnight ferry to Hull. The boat was swarming with boxing fans. They couldn't believe their eyes when they spotted Tyson – no doubt they'd expected him to be flying first class on British Airways – so he was pretty much besieged for the whole crossing. He didn't mind, though, even sharing a few drinks with his supporters, and joining in with the chants and sing-songs out on the deck.

Some of the media were there too, and I found myself standing beside Tyson when he gave an interview to Sky Sports. I'd given him strict instructions to stick to boxing talk – I wanted to keep our baby news under wraps, certainly until the ten-week scan – yet my pleas fell on deaf ears. Within minutes he'd told the reporter I was expecting our third child, and soon everybody knew about it, including many fellow passengers.

'Congratulations about the baby, Paris. You must be so happy!' they said.

'Thanks a lot. We're delighted,' I replied, smiling sweetly, before cursing my blabbermouth husband under my breath.

In the circumstances, I didn't really mind, though. The baby news had added a real spring to Tyson's step, and I knew how much fatherhood meant to him.

When we arrived back home, Tyson's main priority was to spend time with the children. He'd missed them terribly and just wanted to switch off from boxing and be a normal dad for a few days. For the next week or so he turned down any media requests that asked him to go down to London or Manchester, instead allowing short interviews to be filmed at our place. It was Morecambe or nothing.

The following morning, as Tyson rested upstairs, I sat on the sofa with a cup of coffee (and with Prince on my lap) and replayed some of the footage from Düsseldorf. I'd had an urge to watch it again, since most of the action in the ring had passed me by on the night; I'd been far too nervous to take it in. Part of me needed reassurance that the victory had actually happened. Tyson's top-of-the-tree status still hadn't really sunk in, and it all felt very surreal. Watching his performance against Klitschko was a sight to behold, though – it was a masterclass in control and composure – and I felt so proud to be married to this amazing athlete.

The online coverage included a post-fight interview I'd given to Kugan Cassius, a boxing presenter who'd followed Tyson's career for years.

'The world has changed for you both today,' he'd said, as the celebrations continued around us.

'I can't really believe he's the heavyweight champion of the world,' I'd replied, with a beaming smile. 'He always said he was going to do it, for himself and for his family, and now here we are. This is the start of something.'

It certainly was the start of something. As I'd soon find out, it was the start of a two-year nightmare.

CHAPTER FIVE

OUT OF CONTROL

OVER THE YEARS I'd become used to Tyson's mood dipping following a big fight. I'd learned to expect him to mope around the house for a few weeks before the next bout was arranged and a new target was set. But the aftermath of Klitschko v Fury was like nothing I'd ever witnessed before. Once the post-fight euphoria had worn off, within days of returning home to Morecambe, Tyson had sunk into a black hole of darkness and despair. Other boxers might have spent weeks basking in the glory of their world heavyweight champion status, but Tyson did the opposite. He just couldn't find any positives. In his mind, he'd achieved his boyhood dream and there was only one direction for his career to go.

'It's all downhill from here,' he'd say. 'Nothing for me to aim for any more. I'm done. I'm finished.'

'Tyson, that's not true,' I'd reply. 'You've worked so hard for this title, and you've got so much more to offer.'

It was heartbreaking to see him reacting in this way. It was as if that glorious night in Düsseldorf, and those gleaming world title belts, meant absolutely nothing to him.

Tyson's post-fight gloom had been triggered by other things, too, not least the reaction from the British media. Rather than praise a home-grown boxer for an outstanding achievement, some newspapers had chosen to treat him like Public Enemy Number One. Everywhere he turned there were negative headlines and nonsense stories – many linked to interviews he'd given when he was much younger – and Tyson began to sense a real vendetta against him, and maybe even his Traveller background. He wasn't pleading for back-patting and arse-kissing – he knew that his cocky boxing persona wasn't everyone's cup of tea – but he was really dismayed by the lack of credit and recognition.

Then came an online petition calling for Tyson to be removed from the BBC Sports Personality of the Year 2015 nominee list. All the bad press had led to some people taking exception to his inclusion, and there was also a backlash against comments he'd made about fellow candidate, the athlete Jessica Ennis-Hill. Tyson had said she was a brilliant Olympian, who'd achieved great success, and who also looked good in a dress. The media immediately piled on him, accusing him of sexism.

The BBC stood their ground though and kept Tyson on the list, so just before Christmas we attended the awards ceremony at the SSE Arena in Belfast. There were anti-Fury protests outside the venue and, although we didn't see or hear them, I knew this really bothered him. When he was interviewed by Gary Lineker on stage, prior to the final presentation, Tyson made a point of apologising sincerely for any hurt that past comments might have caused. He was voted into fourth place on the night – tennis player Andy Murray came top for the second time – but I wasn't the only person who thought the heavyweight boxing champion of the world deserved to win that award, and had been judged unfairly by the public.

Back home in Morecambe, Tyson's state of mind worsened. He simply couldn't get his head around all this hostility and bad feeling.

'What have I done to deserve all this?' he'd say. 'Why is everybody on my case?'

Adding to his turmoil was a real sense of grief, too. With the Fury v Klitschko circus now over, and with more time to reflect and dwell upon things, I think the death of Uncle Hughie and the miscarriage of our baby had finally begun to sink in. The non-stop fight preparations hadn't allowed Tyson much space to mourn, and those feelings of deep sadness began to rise to the surface. I often found him lying on our bed, sobbing, and instinctively knew what was caus-ing his sorrow. My attempts to comfort him and talk to him usually fell flat – he'd just clam up and bury his face in the pillow – so I'd just close the bedroom door and allow him to grieve alone.

Tyson soon found something to dull his pain. Within days of returning home from Germany he started to drink heav-ily, downing pint after pint in Morecambe's many pubs and getting completely trashed on a nightly basis. While I didn't

the local pubs, and all too often would find my husband slumped in a corner, barely able to move or speak. My feelings would be a mixture of relief (that Tyson was safe), shame (that he was making a fool of himself) and anger (that he was a selfish, thoughtless man-child who didn't give a stuff about his family).

These rescue missions became so commonplace they almost followed a script. Get in the car. Drag Tyson out of a pub. Shove him onto the back seat. Drive him home. Push him through the front door. Read him the riot act.

'Go to bed, Tyson,' I'd say. 'Do not shout. Do not argue. Do not wake up the kids. And clean up your own sick.'

'OK, OK,' he'd slur. 'I get the message . . .'

More often than not, though, he'd throw up all over the carpet. Every single time he'd promise it'd never happen again, but I learned not to believe him.

He didn't sleep well, either. Throughout the night he'd toss and turn and would often wake up, bolt upright, convinced that burglars were trying to break into the house, or that a serial killer was on the loose. It was really frightening to witness, and I'd try my best to calm him down, persuading him that he was just seeing things, or having a bad nightmare. When his anxiety got too much he'd climb out of bed, grab his car keys and wander out of the door.

'It's no use, I can't sleep. I'm going for a drive,' he'd say, ignoring my pleas to stay put. For the next few hours I'd be wide awake, frantic with worry, asking myself all sorts of questions.

Where was he going at this time of night? Where was he escaping to? Was he putting his safety at risk? Was he seeing another woman?

When I rang to check his whereabouts, he'd tell me he was just driving around in circles, going nowhere in particular. He'd return home at 5 a.m., just as the Morecambe Bay seagulls were starting their noisy dawn chorus. While I'd be hugely relieved to hear his key in the lock, I'd feel pretty resentful too. Sleep deprivation was no good for a busy young mother who had a home and kids to look after, and I'd often feel completely wiped out the following day. And not forgetting the fact I was pregnant with our third child. Looking back, I don't know how the hell I coped in the circumstances. It was a definite case of 'needs must'.

My husband's behaviour became more erratic as time went on. I never knew which Tyson I'd be waking up next to. One morning his mood would be so low he'd be unable to drag himself out of bed, yet the next morning he'd be up bright and early, bouncing around the kitchen and pretending all was well with the world. I knew it was a big act, though. I'd lived with him long enough to recognise when his happiness was forced and his smile painted on. These false highs never lasted very long.

A disastrous day trip to a theme park was a case in point.

'It's sunny out there, let's take the kids to Alton Towers,' he'd said one morning. 'We could all do with a nice family day out.'

'Are you sure?' I'd asked him. He'd been on a serious downer for most of the week, and I doubted whether he'd enjoy walking around a theme park swarming with people.

'Course I'm sure. I'll be fine. Let's go.'

So we loaded up the car with excited kids and made the two-hour trip down to Staffordshire. Venezuela and Prince were beside themselves as we passed through the turnstiles and headed towards all the rides and attractions. However, after an hour of all the crowds and the queues (and dozens of selfie requests) Tyson's anxiety levels had hit the roof.

'Paris, I can't stand much more of this,' he whispered to me. 'I need to go home.'

'I knew this would happen,' I said through gritted teeth, 'but you wouldn't listen, would you?'

As Tyson made his way back to the car, it was left to me to explain to the children that Daddy was feeling a bit poorly, and that we had to go back to Morecambe. We'd stop off at McDonalds on the way home for a treat, I told them, and we'd pay a return visit to Alton Towers another day, maybe when it was a little quieter. Prince and Venezuela both burst into tears, of course. We'd only just arrived, and they were having so much fun. I shared their disappointment – I didn't want to go home either – but I couldn't let them know I was as upset as they were.

Shielding the kids from Tyson's issues became my priority, although this wasn't always easy. There were plenty of times when I felt like screaming at the top of my lungs when their father rolled in from the pub in the early hours, but I'd hear my son and daughter stirring in their beds and think, *No, don't go there, Paris. It's really not worth the upset. They mustn't know what's going on.*

There were other occasions when Tyson did a disappearing act for a couple of days – usually a weekend drinking binge, or some unplanned road trip – and the children would naturally ask where he was.

'Daddy's gone to work,' I'd say, while making a mental note to avoid going into the town centre that day. I didn't want the kids catching sight of their father through a pub window, necking down his tenth pint, surrounded by strangers. In those days I found myself doing a lot of sugar-coating, forever trying to gloss over matters for the sake of the family.

Dealing with Tyson was like looking after a child and, as time went on, I began to feel more like his carer than his wife. In fact, coping with the children's challenging behaviour was easier in many ways. I could forgive Prince or Venezuela if they were ever sick on the carpet, because it was usually the result of an illness. I could excuse a bit of mischief and naughtiness from my kids, because that's what kids did. But Tyson was a grown man who was responsible for his own actions, and he pushed my sympathy to the limit.

Tyson's excessive drinking began to drive a wedge between us, and I could feel my resentment growing. He became so wrapped up in himself that he rarely displayed any affection towards me or the kids and, where he'd been so pleased to learn that I was pregnant, now he hardly showed any interest. The fact that a much-wanted third child was due in the summer seemed neither here nor there to him, and it left me feeling ignored and unloved.

In the spring and summer of 2016, Tyson's promotion team had started to set the wheels in motion for a Fury versus Klitschko rematch, which had formed part of the initial deal. They knew Tyson was enjoying some serious 'downtime', though – news of his pub crawls had started to filter through to the media – but the fact they were cracking on with their plans suggested they expected him to snap back and resume training soon. Many boxers took a temporary break from their strict exercise regimes and rigid diet plans after a big fight, so this wasn't ringing alarm bells for them.

I knew otherwise, of course. Behind closed doors, things were much worse than they imagined. Tyson had never been so out of shape, physically and mentally. He was miles away from fitness. He'd begun to seriously pile on the pounds, tipping the scales at twenty-six stone thanks to all the beer he was drinking and all the junk he was eating. Tyson had a real sweet tooth – he loved chocolate, cakes and biscuits – and, when he was home, he'd fill his face like there was no tomorrow. I'd always try to persuade him to eat healthily – at dinnertime I'd prepare us wholesome family meals, like I'd always done – but it was no use. A couple of hours later he'd complain of still being hungry and drive out to get a fish supper or a Chinese takeaway. It seemed he could never satisfy his appetite – he simply didn't know when to stop – and soon his belly became as big as mine, the difference being that his was full of beer, not baby.

A date was finally set for the rematch: Saturday 9 July at the Manchester Arena. Tyson seemed genuinely up for the challenge, but from my perspective he was utterly delusional. I remember sitting in the passenger seat of his car and shaking my head as he chatted to various sports reporters on speakerphone, giving it the usual macho-man trash talk.

'Course I'm ready to face Klitschko again,' he said, believing every word he said. 'I can't wait to defend my title. But it won't be like the last fight. This time he'll get knocked out in round one . . .'

The official 'Fury v Klitschko 2' press conference took place at the Manchester Arena on Wednesday 27 April. The day had got off to a really bad start; Tyson and I had argued with each other because he was acting like a stroppy teenager, refusing to dress smartly, tidy his hair or even have a shave.

'You can't turn up like that, Tyson, you look a total mess,' I'd said, frowning at the crumpled T-shirt and jeans he'd thrown on. 'What will people think?'

'I don't care what people think,' he'd replied. 'There's no point in getting all dressed up. No one gives a damn about me any more.'

The whole event was toe-curling from start to finish. I sat there in the front row, cringing with embarrassment, as my chubby, scruffy husband told the world's boxing media that it was a 'disgrace' for him to be called an athlete, that he was as fat as a pig, and that he'd eaten every pie in Lancashire. Then, just as I'd thought things couldn't get any worse, Tyson stood up, whipped off his T-shirt, grabbed his flabby stomach and began to taunt Klitschko.

'You let a fat man beat you,' he sneered. 'Shame on you.'

Sitting beside him on the stage, Tyson's trainer, Uncle Peter, and his manager, Mick Hennessy, looked absolutely mortified. I felt the same, and just prayed for a trapdoor to open and the ground to swallow me up. My husband was unrecognisable from the flashy showman who, the previous year, had entertained a roomful of reporters with his Batman costume and his snappy soundbites. It broke my heart to see him in such a sorry state.

Photos of Tyson's bare tummy were splashed all over the following day's newspapers – the tabloids lapped it up, of course – and questions were inevitably asked about his desire and commitment, since he'd clearly let himself go. In response, within a few weeks Tyson's team had packed him off to a pre-fight training camp in Holland, where it was hoped he'd lose some pounds, reach his ideal weight, and prove the critics wrong. I had serious doubts, though – in my opinion, he didn't have the self-discipline to go through with it – so it came as no shock to me when everything fell apart at the seams. Tyson hated being in Holland (he said he missed me and the kids, but I reckon he missed the pubs and clubs more) and he just couldn't summon up any enthusiasm to train. Much to my relief the rematch ended up being postponed after Tyson badly injured his ankle. I don't think I was alone in seeing this as a blessing in disguise. With his fragile state of mind, and his serious lack of focus, he'd have been endangering himself by stepping into the ring against a hard-hitting boxer like Klitschko.

By the time June 2016 had arrived the nights were getting light, but Tyson's mood was getting dark. Ever since I'd known him he'd functioned better with a structure to his life, and with a target in his sights, but the fight postponement had left him feeling useless and aimless. He continued to numb his pain by drinking heavily. He spent a crazy night in the French city of Nice during the Euro 2016 football championships, shelling out a fortune on a round of two hundred Jägerbombs for partying England supporters. The next day he was photographed in the media without his shirt, drunkenly singing and chanting with fans in the street. I was less than impressed.

In the cold light of day, back home in Morecambe, he began to openly question his place and purpose in the world. Worryingly, he began to wonder out loud whether his life was worth living.

'What's the point of it all?' he'd say. 'Life means nothing to me any more. Maybe I should just end it all. You and the kids would be much better off without me around.'

'Please don't say things like that, Tyson. I need you, Prince and Venezuela need you, and so will this little one,' I'd say, looking down at my baby bump.

I honestly didn't think he was seriously contemplating suicide, even when, one sunny morning, he told me he was going out for a drive and wasn't coming back. It wasn't the first time he'd walked out with a similar warning hanging in the air, only to stagger home later stinking of beer after another pub session. He'd seemed a little more upset than normal on this particular day, though – his eyes had looked really sad and heavy – and I'd felt really uneasy as he'd stepped out of the front door, climbed into his red Ferrari and zoomed off.

A few hours passed and I heard nothing from Tyson (ordinarily he'd call me two or three times per day) so I rang him. No reply. I kept redialling and redialling; still no reply. With my concerns mounting, I called his father.

'John, have you spoken to Tyson today?'

'No, I've not. Is everything OK?'

'He said some silly things this morning and he's driven off and not come back. I'm getting a bit worried.'

'That doesn't sound good, Paris. Give Shane a call. He might have heard from him. Let me do some ring-rounds too, and I'll keep you posted.'

But there'd been no contact with his brother, either, and as night fell, with still no sign of Tyson, I was getting frantic. I had no idea what to do for the best; I was heavily pregnant with two young kids running around, so I couldn't leave the house. It was pointless jumping into my car and searching for him, in any case – he could have driven to Land's End for all I knew – and, as I paced around the front room and peered through the window, I became panic-stricken.

Just as I was about to call the police, at around 7 p.m., Tyson walked through the door, his face as white as a sheet. He looked in shock, and seemed extremely jittery. I dashed over and flung my arms around him.

'Where the hell have you been?' I demanded, crying tears of relief. 'I've been trying to get hold of you all day. I've been worried sick.'

'I was going to drive my car into a bridge,' he said, his voice trembling, 'but then a voice told me not to do it.'

'Oh my God,' I gasped, as my stomach lurched. 'What on earth came over you?'

'I don't know, Paris. I really don't know. I'm so sorry.'

It turned out that Tyson had been speeding along the fast lane of the motorway, and had been gripped by a sudden impulse to veer off the road. Within seconds of putting his foot down, a voice in his head had urged him to think about his children, and – thank goodness – he'd managed to stop in his tracks and had skidded to a halt.

As he told me what happened, with tears rolling down his cheeks, I just didn't know what to think. I felt incredibly sad that he'd had these suicidal thoughts, yet – if I'm being brutally honest – I felt really angry, too. I was furious that he could even contemplate leaving his wife without a husband and his kids without a father, including our unborn baby. I couldn't process it. I couldn't understand it. We had two beautiful children. We had great friends and family. We had a lovely home. We had money in the bank. We had each other. Why wasn't this enough for him? Why didn't he want to live?

I'd later learn how depressive illness affects individuals from all walks of life, regardless of status or background, and how, in severe cases, it can detach people from all sense of reality. But, at that point in time – and without that knowledge or context – I just saw Tyson as an incredibly self-centred, self-destructive person who, in a moment of madness, had been willing to wreck our family unit. The bridge incident convinced me even more that the only person who could solve his problems, and turn his life around, was Tyson himself. I could try to do the right thing, and say the right words, but I couldn't control his thoughts or actions. His destiny, good or bad, was in his own hands.

I also had some decisions to make about my own future.

There had been times, particularly in the early part of 2016, when I'd thought about leaving Tyson. Life with a binge-eating beer-monster who didn't give a crap about his wife and kids was horrendous, so there were many occasions when I'd felt like doing a runner.

I can't do this anymore . . . I'd say to myself. *I just can't deal with this* . . .

Sometimes I'd sit at the kitchen table with a cup of tea and daydream about packing my suitcase, bundling the kids into the car and escaping to my parents' place. I didn't feel in any personal danger – Tyson channelled all his anger and aggression towards himself, never the children and me – but I just craved some peace, quiet and normality. Living with

Tyson was so challenging and exhausting, physically and emotionally, and I needed a break.

However, once he'd started to talk about suicide, I shelved any ideas of a quick exit. Tyson was so vulnerable – the bridge episode had demonstrated that – and, since he hadn't stopped his wild drinking, he was clearly a risk to himself. I reckoned he'd definitely end up dead if I left him to his own devices – smashing into a wall, giving himself alcohol poisoning or choking on his own vomit – and I wasn't prepared to let that happen, or to live with the guilt that would follow. While I knew I couldn't cure Tyson of his self-destructive feelings, I wasn't ready to bail on him or let him crash and burn.

I felt a deep sense of loyalty and responsibility towards him, too. He may have been a drunken dosser, but he was *my* drunken dosser and, as his wife, I saw it as my duty to stick to my marriage vows and support him for better or for worse, and in sickness and in health. There were some days when I hated him but, by the same token, I never stopped loving him. Despite all the dark days, I was still convinced there was light at the end of the tunnel.

Rightly or wrongly, I also decided to battle through these troubles alone. I chose not to confide in any of my friends and family about Tyson's issues, even though most of them knew he'd gone off the rails. Looking back, there was a definite sense of denial on my part. If I didn't mention the situation I could almost pretend it wasn't real, and if I didn't open up they wouldn't be able to tell me things I didn't want to hear. Had I gone on a girls' night out and revealed how despairing I felt, I know exactly how they'd have responded; they'd have echoed my own advice to them had the roles been reversed.

'How can he behave like that, when he's got a wife and family to look after?'

'He's not worth the trouble. Dump him, and start afresh.'

'Time to put you and the kids first. Pack your bags and leave.'

More to the point, I was also hugely embarrassed by Tyson's careless and irresponsible behaviour. Most of my friends were fellow Travellers, and family values were the bedrock of our community – running a happy and settled home was central to our culture – and I felt ashamed that I'd ended up with a problem drinker who preferred whisky to his wife and partying to parenting. I was too proud to admit that my marriage had lost its way and that my husband was spiralling out of control.

There was another reason I kept things to myself, too. Depression was rarely discussed in Gypsy circles, in common with many other parts of society. Growing up at Tilts Farm, mental health issues had often been brushed under the carpet – I remember being told that neighbours had 'bad nerves' or were 'under the weather' – and, even twenty years later, it was still a taboo subject among the Traveller community. I was ill-equipped to recognise Tyson's illness for what it was. I could see he was poorly, but I struggled to understand the reasons behind his behaviour. I found it really hard to put things into words.

I never discussed Tyson's problems with my own family, either – I just didn't feel up to it – but they weren't daft. Mam in particular realised we were having serious issues ('I knew all along, Paris, but you wouldn't let me help you,' she'd later say when we finally talked things through). She frequently offered to look after the children, though – it was her way of letting me know that she was there for me – but I rarely took her up on it. Tyson was hardly ever at home, and acted distantly when he was, so Prince and Venezuela were often my only company and I wanted them all to myself. My children provided me with the love and affection that Tyson couldn't – they were like my comfort blanket – and caring for them took my mind off all the surrounding chaos. Their presence also served as a reminder that I had to stay positive and had to keep going, for their sakes.

Putting on an act in public could be exhausting, though. Sometimes the stress would mount, the mask would slip, and my emotions would rise to the surface. One such incident took place at a Morecambe pub in the summer of 2016. To most families, going out for a traditional Sunday dinner was a nice way to spend time together. Tyson, however, used it as an excuse to meet up with people for an all-day drinking binge. Straight after we'd eaten our meal he'd throw me his car keys, telling me to go home with the kids and promising to catch up with me later. 'Later' usually meant him stumbling home at two or three in the morning, sometimes at breakfast time if he'd found a lock-in at another bar.

This rigmarole went on, week after week, until one particular Sunday. Tyson had yet again sent me away from the pub, and I was walking through the car park with a friend I'd not known for very long, when I just completely broke down in tears.

'I don't know what to do . . . I just don't know what to do,' I cried. 'This is my life, every day, every week, and I don't think I can cope much longer. Tyson's never out of the pub. He just drinks and drinks. He doesn't care about me or the kids. He hardly talks to me. I feel so hurt, so alone . . .'

The poor woman probably didn't know what to do with this blubbering blond wreck, bless her. It felt good to let off some steam to someone, though, and to release some of the pressure that had been building up for months and months.

The next morning, I'd calmed myself down and regained my composure. While Tyson was sleeping off his hangover I'd sat in the back garden, breathing in the salty sea air, and had taken a few moments to reflect on something my mam had told me when I was a young girl.

'A mother is the backbone of the family,' she'd said. 'For everything else to function, she has to stay strong.'

Those words had always stayed with me, and now they seemed more relevant than ever.

Prince Tyson Luke – named after his dad, of course – was born in July 2016. Tyson and I were both delighted to welcome his safe arrival, but it had marked the end of a very strange pregnancy for me. The joy of carrying a child had been completely overshadowed by my husband's issues and, unlike my previous pregnancies, I'd not felt remotely spoilt or pampered. There'd certainly been no bubble baths or foot massages this time round.

I'd also been kept busy with a big house move. Having outgrown our bungalow, we'd found ourselves a lovely new home at the other end of town, a spacious five-bedroomed detached house with fantastic views across Morecambe Bay. It was in need of renovation – it needed a new roof and windows, and the interior needed painting and plastering – but, to me, it was the perfect property for our growing family. I crossed my fingers that this upgrade, and our beautiful new baby, would mark a new and happier chapter for the Furys; maybe Tyson would want to stay at home more now, I hoped, and be less likely to run off to the pub.

But only a few weeks after giving birth, I found myself back in hospital, and this time it wasn't baby-related. I'd received a phone call from our friend Dave, telling me that Tyson had experienced a frightening episode while sitting in his Ferrari. As he'd tried to start the car his whole body had lost its ability to function; he couldn't even turn the key in the ignition. He'd gone into panic mode, before contacting his best pal to come to his aid. Tyson had been very distressed and disorientated when Dave had found him, complaining that his heart was racing, so they'd both gone to the nearest hospital to get him checked out.

I quickly organised for Shannon to look after the kids, then jumped in the car and dashed to the hospital. I arrived to find Tyson in a private ward, looking ashen and shaken, with Dave, John senior and Shane by his bedside, all looking very concerned. But the instant Tyson saw me he sat up straight and, much to everyone's shock, started ranting and raving.

'I've had a heart attack!' he yelled. 'My heart rate's gone through the roof. My body seized up. I couldn't drive the car. I'm too young to die, Paris, *I'm too young to die . . .*'

I tried to respond – 'Calm down, Tyson, just calm down . . .' – but he wouldn't listen and just carried on shouting. I'd never seen him so worked up and agitated. Something was wrong. Something was very, very wrong.

'Everyone here's trying to kill me,' he continued. 'I know Dave wants to murder me. The doctors are trying to poison me. And I bet *you* want me dead, too, Paris . . .'

'What are you saying?' I said. 'Stop this, please . . .'

This was too much. It was a living nightmare. Tyson was spouting hurtful nonsense and was clearly in the middle of some kind of breakdown. He needed help beyond anything I or the family could provide, and it was about time we got some expert medical advice. Fortunately, a consultant was on hand to put us in the picture. He studied Tyson's notes and explained that his symptoms in the car had pointed towards a severe anxiety attack – patients can often mistake them for heart trouble – and he'd been given some medication to settle him down and reduce his stress levels. The consultant also told me that Tyson's disturbing outbursts were the result of paranoid delusions. This was quite a worrying development, he said, and he'd need to be referred to a mental health practitioner for a detailed assessment.

'He'll get a proper diagnosis that way, Mrs Fury,' said the doctor.

'Thank you,' I replied, relieved that I seemed to be finally getting somewhere. 'I just need to know what's going on.'

Following a twelve-hour stay, Tyson was discharged from hospital in a much calmer state. He'd been given some sleeping pills to help him relax at night, and had been signposted to his GP for an appointment. In typically rash fashion, however, one of the first things he did after returning home was to book a last-minute family holiday.

'We need to get away from all this,' said Tyson, 'so I've booked us a nice hotel in Cannes for ten days.'

'Is this really a good idea?' I asked, worried that he'd not recovered properly from his panic attack. He persuaded me that some Riviera sunshine would do us the world of good, so I washed our clothes and packed our bags and, later that week, we all flew out to France.

The holiday was a calamity from start to finish. For the first three nights, Tyson refused to take his sleeping pills – he was convinced they contained poison – and, as a result, he stayed awake and anxious from dusk until dawn. On the fourth night he agreed to take one, but this wiped him out for the following day. I was left to organise and entertain three kids on my own – taking them to the beach was a pretty exhausting experience – while Tyson slept on. By day five he was complaining of feeling dreadful, both in mind and in body, and it became quite clear our holiday was a write-off. We had no option but to pack up our things and fly back home.

'I'm so sorry, Paris,' he said as we headed to the airport. 'I don't know what's wrong with me.'

'Tyson, it's not your fault,' I replied, feeling genuinely concerned for him. 'We'll get to the bottom of it, don't you worry.'

A few weeks after our return, and following various tests and assessments, a GP was finally able to give Tyson his diagnosis: bipolar disorder and obsessive compulsive disorder. Being bipolar explained his severe mood swings, which could veer from artificial highs to suicidal lows, and the OCD explained his deeply fixated behaviour, which, at different stages of his life, had presented itself via obsessive training or obsessive drinking. Receiving professional help, and being able to put a name to his issues, did so much to help him make sense of things. While he didn't want to be ill, at least he now knew that his personal obstacles and challenges could be linked to recognised mental conditions.

I was massively relieved by Tyson's diagnosis, too. Finally, I had some answers. While all these medical terms were new to me – I'd never heard of bipolar or OCD before – at least I could try to begin to understand his feelings and behaviours. It felt good to finally get some clarity after months of confusion.

Tyson remained unconvinced that prescribed medication was the right route for him, though. While he was prepared to have occasional therapy sessions with a psychologist, he was fearful that once he started taking pills he'd be on them forever. He felt confident that, in time, he'd be able to draw upon his inner strength – and that famous winning mentality of his – to lift himself out of the doldrums and start living normally again. Both he and I were under no illusions, though. This was no quick fix. Tyson was still very ill – he continued to eat and drink to excess – and his recovery wouldn't happen overnight. But by seeking help and getting a diagnosis, he'd made the first small step on a long and bumpy journey.

With all the concerns for Tyson's poor mental health, it became inevitable that the Fury v Klitschko rematch would have to be scrapped. In September 2016, his management team released a statement declaring him medically unfit to fight.

'Tyson will now immediately undergo the treatment he needs to make a full recovery,' it said. Finally, the world knew the true extent of his illness.

I braced myself for the fallout. Tyson was naturally devastated. In his mind the fight cancellation signalled the end of his boxing career, and he convinced himself he'd never compete professionally again. I didn't believe this, though. Despite all his woes I knew he wasn't finished in the ring, and I was convinced that, one fine day, he'd come back fighting. Boxing was his life. It was in his blood. He loved the sport too much to abandon it. For me, it wasn't a case of *if* he'd return; it was a case of *how* he'd return.

But Tyson wouldn't be told; he'd brush off my 'you can do it' pep talks and he seemed to lose all faith in himself. I remember him getting some car insurance forms returned, because the firm had queried his job description. We owned a couple of mobile home companies at the time and, in the 'Occupation' section, Tyson had written 'Business Manager'. This wasn't an attempt to get cheaper insurance, it just reflected his own perception of his status. I thought he was being ridiculous.

'Oh, for God's sake, Tyson, just put down "professional boxer".'

'But I'm not, though, am I? It's not my job anymore. I haven't fought for months, and I'll never fight again.'

That same autumn, the family relocated to Cheshire for a few weeks. Our new house was getting renovated, and there was paint and plaster flying everywhere, so Tyson and I got a trailer and pitched it next to his dad's house in Styal village. Although I hadn't lived in a caravan for five years, and had got quite used to the creature comforts of central heating and proper plumbing, I quite fancied the idea of going back to basics and reconnecting with our Gypsy roots. I also thought it would be good for the kids (the older two, at least) to sample some traditional Traveller life and learn more about their culture.

There was another motive behind the move. I was desperate to get Tyson out of Morecambe for a while. Despite his diagnosis his partying continued, and he turned a blind eye to my protests and objections. By living nearer to his dad and brothers, I thought, he might just change his ways. Tyson's true friends, like Dave, had stopped drinking in his company to try to discourage him – that's how caring they were – but there were still plenty of people around town who'd do the exact opposite.

In hindsight, moving to Styal was possibly the worst decision I could have made. The village was close to the social honeypots of Wilmslow and Alderley Edge – both renowned for their swanky pubs and clubs – and, despite my efforts to keep him indoors, Tyson just replaced Lancashire nights out with Cheshire nights out. He found a whole new set of hangers-on to drink with and, as I'd soon learn, would start to get his kicks via other means.

Tyson's brothers had always been so supportive of him, but even they became increasingly dismayed by his unruly behaviour. Like many of his friends, they eventually stopped socialising with him because, after a bellyful of drinks, he was no fun to be with. John Boy once rang me, really upset, because a club-goer had filmed a worse-for-wear Tyson on their phone and posted it online. Seeing the world heavyweight champion staggering around, looking all puffy and bloated, was so painful to watch.

'What on earth is he on?' said John Boy. 'He's totally out of his brain.'

'It's too much alcohol,' I replied. 'He's been drinking for two days solid.'

'You've got to rein him in, Paris. Keep him inside, don't let him out.'

'Well, I'd like to see *you* tying down a six-foot-nine, twenty-six-stone man. But I get your drift, John. This is getting ridiculous.'

In October 2016, however, the family's concern for Tyson's well-being went into overdrive. Our world came crashing down in dramatic fashion when news broke of Tyson testing positive for cocaine during a random anti-doping test he'd had to take. To add insult to injury, he'd also revealed in an interview for *Rolling Stone* magazine that he'd been regularly using cocaine to try to combat his depression. I only became aware of all this when I saw a headline on a newspaper stand – it literally stopped me in my tracks – and I automatically assumed there'd been a terrible mistake. Tyson had been anti-drugs all his life. He never dreamed of sniffing or smoking a strange substance. He used to tell me that druggies and dealers were the lowest of the low.

'Boxing is my only addiction,' he'd always said. 'Drugs are for dossers.'

The facts didn't lie though, and me, John and the brothers all met up in Styal for a crisis meeting with Tyson. At first he tried to deny everything – he'd clearly not seen the media coverage, having been in the pub all day – but when he realised the news was out there in black and white, he could sense the game was up. Boiling with rage, I let rip.

'So this is what you've been doing every night, is it?' I shouted. 'You're a druggie as well as a drunk, then? What kind of slinks have *you* been mixing with? What kind of role model are you to your children, eh?'

Tyson didn't say a word. He was so ashamed he could hardly lift up his head. He looked like a naughty little schoolboy who'd just been caught out.

His dad and his brothers wiped the floor with him. I'd never seen them so angry and upset. Shane, the brother who was closest in age to Tyson, was utterly heartbroken.

'I can't believe you've been doing drugs,' he said over and over again, shaking his head in disappointment.

Tyson's alcohol issues had been hard enough for us to deal with, but adding Class A drugs to the mix had brought real shame to the family, and had gone against everything in our respectable Traveller culture. Never having known anyone who'd taken cocaine, I hadn't been able to see the signs.

I'd never felt so let down in my life – it truly felt like the final straw – and I wondered whether our marriage could survive this huge setback. But, like I'd done so many times before, I told myself to sit tight and ride the storm. I just wasn't prepared to give up on him, for his own sake and our family's sake. I still loved him. The kids still loved him. And I was pretty sure that he still loved us, too.

I knew the drugs situation would be bad news for his boxing career, though. And sure enough, by the time we'd moved back to our house in Morecambe, the British Boxing Board of Control had suspended Tyson's boxing licence. It was bombshell news and he took it as badly as I'd expected. It marked a new low for him – there'd been plenty of those that year – and sank him even further into depression. I'd often find him crying as he sang along to one of his favourite country songs, 'Wine into Water', which told the story of a hopeless alcoholic whose wayward behaviour had hurt his loved ones, and who'd found himself begging God for salvation.

As Tyson's deep voice filled the air, full of pain and sorrow, my own tears would start to fall. That same voice had serenaded me in a boxing ring and one day, God willing, it would serenade me again.

CHAPTER SIX

ROAD TO RECOVERY

In the spring of 2017 I discovered I was expecting again, less than a year after giving birth to Baby Tyson. Having once struggled to conceive, it seemed my pregnancies were now coming along like buses, in quick succession. I was thrilled, of course – the more kids the merrier – but that still didn't stop me worrying how I'd cope with two children so close together. The elder two – Venezuela and Prince – were now both attending primary school, which helped matters, but I was still a little concerned.

'You'll be fine, Paris,' said Mam when I told her my baby news. 'You'll take it in your stride. You've done brilliantly with the other three kids.'

'Four, including Tyson,' I replied.

Tyson's spirits were momentarily lifted by the glad tidings – he gave me a big hug, happy that we were building that big family we'd always wanted – and Prince and Venezuela were very excited about a little brother or sister. Like my previous pregnancy, however, I didn't get much chance to enjoy that special time in my life because Tyson was still so unwell. The official diagnosis of OCD and bipolar disorder, although very useful, hadn't been a magic bullet. And, while he paid occasional visits to a psychologist, he still wasn't convinced he was cut out for that type of therapy. He felt very strongly his recovery would stem from his own deeds and actions rather than another person's words and advice. It was nice to see a flash of the same iron will that had helped him hit the boxing heights.

His private battle had now become public, too. After the release of the *Rolling Stone* interview, and the media storm that followed, the whole world now knew about Tyson Fury's depression and addiction. In days gone by I might have been embarrassed to see our personal lives being splashed all over the tabloids but, by the time the article had been published, towards the end of 2016, I no longer worried what people thought. In fact, I felt relieved, not ashamed, that everything was finally out in the open. Going public might help Tyson to come to terms with his illness, I reckoned, and might make him realise he wasn't alone. Many fellow sufferers had got in touch to offer support and advice – including some very famous celebrities – and he'd often get stopped in the street by kindly well-wishers who'd read the stories in the papers and sympathised with his plight. Also, judging by what I saw and heard in the media, he was earning a lot of respect for tackling such a sensitive subject. By opening up about the hardest fight of his life – against his own inner demons – Tyson had delivered a stark but important message: even the most physically strong men in the world could be mentally vulnerable.

Tyson's *Rolling Stone* revelations had lessened my burden, too, because I could finally stop hiding from reality. Papering over the cracks and pretending that everything was fine had tired me out, and it felt liberating to finally drop the big act and admit that Tyson was very poorly, and that our family life had suffered. No longer would I have to make excuses for the events he failed to attend, or the calls he never returned, or the people he let down, because everyone now knew about his mental health struggles. I was the one person who'd borne the brunt of Tyson's issues and challenges, and it felt like a huge weight had been lifted off my shoulders.

Tyson's day-to-day well-being continued to be a worry, though. Thanks to his excessive eating, drinking and loung- ing he ballooned to twenty-nine stone, a massive ten stone over his fighting weight. None of his clothes fitted – he had to buy a whole new wardrobe of XXXL gear – and he became, in his own words, 'a heart attack waiting to happen'. Tyson's physical decline frightened me to death. I was more concerned about his underlying health than his outward appearance – I loved him unconditionally, whatever his size – and urged him to lose a few stones. I suspected this weight gain was hurting him inside, too. Each time he stepped on the scales, or squeezed into a T-shirt, he probably felt himself getting further and further away from the sport he adored.

Sometimes, in response to my concerns, Tyson would tell me he was cleaning up his act and that he planned to watch his diet and get on the treadmill. These best intentions rarely lasted, though. The stress of it all would trigger his anxiety.

To make himself feel better he'd comfort-eat or binge-drink, and would find himself back at square one.

When things got too much for me I'd sometimes ring Shane for a chat. Coping with Tyson on my own, when his extended family were back in Cheshire, could feel very lonely and isolating.

'I just don't know what to do with him, Shane. It's one step forward, three steps back at the moment.'

'Listen, you're doing all you can,' he'd reply. 'I'll try and pop over to see Tyson this week sometime. In the meantime, try and stay positive, Paris. I know it's hard, but it's not going to be like this forever.'

He was right. I had to stay upbeat, and take heart from the occasional glimpses of the Tyson of old. Now and then I'd see him playing with the kids in the garden, or punching the air when Manchester United scored a winner, and I'd dare to dream he was turning a corner. But, more often than not, the following day reality would slap me in the face and bring me crashing down to earth. I'd be getting the older kids ready for school, and feeding the baby his breakfast, and making a list for the weekly Asda shop – a typical multitasking morning – and I'd get a phone call from Tyson while he walked along the beach, telling me over and over again how he hated himself, how he'd lost all hope, and how his life wasn't worth living.

The bad cop voice in my head would pipe up first.

I'm about to do the school run. I've got the big shop to do before Baby Tyson gets hungry. I've got the whole house to clean when I get back, and a family dinner to prepare. And I'm pregnant, and I'm hormonal and I'm tired. But, yet again, it's all about YOU . . .

But then my good cop voice would take over, reminding me that Tyson was suffering with severe mental illness. If he was going to make any kind of recovery, he needed my support, sympathy and understanding, no matter how difficult that sometimes felt. As a couple we'd gone through so much together – the lows, the highs, the in-betweens – and I just needed to persevere, and keep that hope afloat.

Keep listening to him, Paris. Keep telling him you love him. Keep believing that better days lie ahead.

It was Halloween 2017, and I was busy putting Prince and Venezuela to bed. I'd taken them out trick-or-treating around the neighbourhood (something Tyson had always done before, when he was well) and they'd had a great time filling up their swag-bags with all sorts of goodies. Meanwhile, Tyson was getting himself ready for a Halloween party at a local pub, the sort of occasion that usually ended up with him rolling home in the early hours, drunk as a skunk.

He emerged from our bedroom wearing a skintight, glow-in-the-dark skeleton suit with a matching mask and a huge pair of black wellies. I just shook my head and sighed. He looked ridiculous. Had Tyson been in a good place, this fancy dress costume might have made me laugh. But he wasn't in a good place, and all I felt was pity. I just saw a grown man acting like a kid. A champion boxer acting like a clown.

'Have a good night, then,' I said, flatly. 'Just keep the noise down when you get in. I don't want you waking up the children.'

'I'll try my best. See you later,' he replied, before picking up his wallet and heading outdoors.

With the kids safely tucked up and sleeping soundly, I spent the rest of the evening chilling out watching *Friends*. However, just as I was about to go upstairs to bed, at about 9 p.m., I heard the front door creaking open. For a moment my heart was in my mouth, thinking it was an intruder – I had the Halloween jitters – but, when a six-foot-nine skeleton wandered in, I realised it was my husband.

'Wow, you're back early,' I said. 'Rubbish night, was it? Or did you get chucked out?'

There followed a long pause, before Tyson's eyes began to brim with tears.

'I can't live like this any more, Paris. I'm done with it all. I've got to make a change. I'm going to start training tomorrow.'

While I felt incredibly sorry for him – he looked so miserable, with beer stains all over his skeleton outfit – I didn't really believe him, either. This wasn't the first time he'd trotted out the 'training tomorrow' line, so I'd learned to take most things he said with a pinch of salt.

Tyson went on to describe what had just happened in the pub, and why he'd decided to come back early. Leaning against the bar in his silly outfit, surrounded by partygoers in their teens, he'd suddenly realised how out of place he looked.

I'm twenty-nine. I'm a husband and a father. What am I doing here with all these youngsters? he'd thought to himself. *Is this really what I want from life?*

Then, in a moment of clarity – he said it felt like an epiphany – he'd put down his pint, walked out of the pub and came straight home.

And here he was, standing in the front room, looking as sad as I'd ever seen him. He told me he needed some time to himself – he seemed so lost and confused – and he went upstairs to the bedroom. After twenty minutes-or-so I went to check on him, and what I witnessed will live with me forever. Tyson had taken off his costume and was kneeling at the end of our bed, his forehead resting on his clasped hands, his body shaking with sobs. He was having a conversation with God, asking for His forgiveness and His guidance. Tyson had always clung on to his faith – even in the depths of depression – and now, in his moment of need, he was begging for help.

'Lord, I can't do this alone,' he cried. 'I need You to help me through.'

My first impulse was to go and give Tyson a big cuddle, but something told me to let him be, and to leave him alone in his prayer. I only returned to the bedroom once I knew he was sleeping peacefully.

The following morning, I woke up early to find a space next to me in the bed. No Tyson. I immediately panicked – then thought he must have just gone for a drive around Morecambe, which he often did when he was anxious – but just as I calmed myself I heard someone moving about downstairs.

I found Tyson in the kitchen, dressed in a tracksuit, filling up a water bottle. He looked up, gave me a big smile, and told me he was going training with his mate Dave – they'd be popping over to the gym across the road – and he'd be back home later for some lunch.

'That sounds great, Tyson,' I said, giving him a hug and a kiss, while trying not to look too surprised. I still felt a little cynical. His enthusiasm was just too good to be true.

But then Tyson did the same thing the next day: up early, training kit on, off to the gym. And the next day. And the next. Was he finally turning the corner? Had the Halloween incident shocked him into action? Or was this more wishful thinking on my part? I decided to have a quiet word with Dave, to gauge his opinion. He'd been such a loyal friend to Tyson over the years. He was as keen as me to get his big buddy back on track and, even though he was no fan of the gym himself, he was prepared to lift some weights or work a stopwatch if it assisted Tyson's recovery. That's what mates were for, he said.

'So what d'you reckon, Dave? Is he serious or what?'

'I can see a spark in him, Paris, a spring in his step. I honestly think he's up for it.'

'God, I hope you're right.'

'Yep, me too. Fingers crossed.'

Tyson stuck faithfully to his daily training routine for the next couple of weeks, spending hours in the gym with

Dave and going for long runs around Morecambe. He changed his drinking and eating habits, too, cutting out the booze and the Big Macs and embracing a much healthier lifestyle. He even began to talk about reviving his boxing career, having spent the last two years telling everyone he was done with the sport. While it was great to see him so optimistic, I warned him to take one step at a time.

'Your health has to come first, Tyson,' I told him. 'You can't get on the comeback trail until you're well enough.'

'I know, I know,' he said. 'I just haven't felt this good in ages.'

Throughout November I sensed his mood stabilising – there were fewer crazy highs and crashing lows – and his behaviour on the whole became more balanced and predictable. I was no longer on tenterhooks every time he went out in the car, for instance, and I felt more comfortable leaving him home alone for a couple of hours. Not only that, I didn't have to guess which version of my husband I'd wake up next to each morning: downbeat Tyson who wanted to stay in bed all day, or upbeat Tyson who wanted to drive to France and back. He was definitely on a more even keel.

He became increasingly engaged with the family, too. Slowly but surely, we started to do ordinary, day-to-day stuff that had previously been impossible, like taking the kids to the local park or going on a shopping trip to Manchester. I could feel the bond between us beginning to strengthen

– we were talking more, and laughing more – and for the first time in two years I felt like his wife again, not his babysitter.

That month we'd welcomed another person into our household, too. Coming to live with us on a temporary basis was Ben Davison, a talented young boxing coach from London who Tyson had met at a Marbella training camp set up for his friend Billy Joe Saunders. Following his Halloween turnaround Tyson had done a great deal of thinking and, as he'd weighed up his future options, he'd made the tough decision to part company with his trainer, Uncle Peter. It was a sad situation – Peter had played a huge part in Tyson's success – but this felt like a big new chapter, and it was probably time for a change.

Ben agreed to help Tyson rediscover his fitness, with a view to staging a boxing comeback when, and if, the time was right. So one afternoon he'd turned up on our doorstep, carrying a huge holdall. Not that I'd received any prior warning of his arrival, of course.

'Oh, Paris, I forgot to tell you. This is Ben, my new trainer,' said Tyson, grinning, ushering him in through the front door. 'I told him it would be OK if he came to live with us for a while, to keep me on the straight and narrow.'

I couldn't help but laugh. It was a good job I was easy-going. To be honest, I think I'd have let Jack the Ripper come and live with us if it meant Tyson getting better.

'Come in, Ben, make yourself at home,' I said. 'I'll put the kettle on.'

Not only was Ben a lovely lad – we treated him like one of the family – he really clicked with Tyson. He took time to understand the hardships he'd gone through, mentally and physically, and explained how, with the right training programme, he'd get him back to full fitness and, more importantly, back feeling happy. With Tyson still massively overweight, Ben must have wondered what he'd signed himself up for; the task ahead was huge, in every sense. Outwardly, though, he appeared up for the challenge and, in my opinion, was the kind of glass-half-full person that Tyson needed.

Most nights, when I finally got the kids to bed (Ben soon adapted to our noisy, chaotic household) the three of us would have kitchen-table discussions, much of them about Tyson's future. One night, Ben suggested it might be a good idea for Tyson to relocate to Marbella for the rest of the winter. By leaving the UK for a couple of months he'd be able to focus solely on the task in hand, and would also benefit from the brilliant boxing facilities over there, including the famous MTK Marbella gym. The Costa del Sol's mild climate and sunny skies would also massively lift his spirits, Ben reckoned.

Tyson would only agree to the move if the family came along, too – me, Prince and Venezuela had travelled around Europe with him in the past – but this time I had to put the kibosh on yet another one of his crazy ideas.

'You can have the baby in Spain, can't you?' he said. 'We could find a decent hospital, and—'

'No chance, Tyson,' I said, putting him straight. 'I can't travel in this state, and there's no way I'm giving birth in a strange place.'

I got my own way, thank goodness. Our second daughter, Valencia (we gave her the middle name of Amber, after Tyson's mam) was born in Lancaster, on 4 December 2017. She arrived two weeks early – but safely and soundly – and her doting parents were thrilled beyond belief.

'My little angel was born this morning,' Tyson posted on Twitter, with a cute photo of our newborn dressed in a pink outfit. 'Thank God and @parisfury1 for this blessing.'

We loaded up the car with the children – as well as all our clothes, toys and Tyson's boxing equipment – and started on our three-day drive to Spain. We had so much stuff (including some in a second car that Ben and Tyson's brother Hughie took) that flying wasn't an option for us, even if Valencia had been old enough. Some of my friends thought I was nuts to even consider a car journey to Spain, with three small kids and a newborn, but for me it was no big deal. I happily got on with it. I'd spent all my married life slotting into Tyson's busy schedule, often dropping everything and making last-minute arrangements to travel to fight camps and boxing venues whenever I got the call.

This time, however, before we set off Ben and I had chatted privately about our concerns for Tyson. Although his attitude was generally good, this trip to Marbella was a big step for him – he'd not trained abroad for years – and we were worried his nerves would kick in as soon as he left Morecambe, and he'd get cold feet and change his mind. With no boxing on the agenda he'd spent much more time at home than usual, and we were scared he might suffer some separation anxiety.

'The most important thing is to keep him in the car and just get him there,' said Ben. 'Once he's arrived, he'll stay put and stick to the training, I'm sure of it.'

'I get it. I'll keep an eye on him.'

Our worries were justified. There were couple of moments along the route when Tyson had a real wobble. The first came as we approached the turn-off at Folkestone, where we were due to connect with the Eurotunnel.

'I've got a bad feeling about this,' said Tyson. 'Maybe we should turn round.'

With Ben's advice ringing in my ears, it was time for some tough love. I felt a bit harsh – I could understand him feeling overwhelmed – but needs must.

'No, Tyson, we're not turning back. You can't drag me and four kids down here for nothing. Ben thinks this is the best plan of action, and you need to put your trust in him.'

A few hours later, having made the crossing over to France, he faltered again when we passed road signs for Paris. I could sense his mood change.

'Can't we just call it quits and go to Disneyland Paris for a holiday?' he asked. The kids would love it, wouldn't they?'

'Drive on, Tyson,' I said, as calmly and firmly as I could. 'Keep focused on the road ahead.'

And, to his credit, he did.

*　　*　　*

A thousand miles later – following three hotel stops numerous wee-stops, nappy-changing stops and baby-feeding stops – Team Fury finally arrived in Marbella on New Year's Eve. Our mission impossible – to physically get Tyson from A to B – was complete. For the next two months, home for me, Tyson, Ben and the children would be a spacious apartment on the outskirts of the city, with indoor and outdoor pools and a lovely sun terrace. Hughie stayed with us for ten days or so, before returning home to the UK.

Tyson's new fitness and wellness regime at the Marbella gym started straight away. He trained every day, between 9 a.m. and 5 p.m., and I made him his breakfast beforehand and his evening meal afterwards. It felt like he was pressing a huge reset button, wiping the slate clean. First off, Ben put him on a fat-burning ketogenic diet, which focused on wholesome, low-carb foods, meaning lots of meat, fish and leafy vegetables. Working in tandem with the eating plan was a structured, timetabled training programme designed by Ben, which alternated between circuits in the gym, runs in the mountains and sparring in the ring. I wasn't there to see Tyson wrapping his hands and pulling on a pair of boxing gloves for the first time in two years, but I can only imagine how amazing that must have felt for him. There'd been plenty of times when he'd doubted it would ever happen.

As soon as a disciplined routine was reintroduced into Tyson's daily life, with a clear set of aims and objectives, his outlook totally altered. It was almost as if he'd replaced one addiction with another. Instead of going to the pub, he headed for the gym. Instead of thinking about his next pint, he focused on his next workout. Instead of craving junk food, he buzzed off running and sparring. Exercise became his medicine and his therapy. It made him feel good, it made him feel valued, and it gave him a brand new zest for life.

And with Tyson's new active, clean-living lifestyle came the weight loss. He set himself realistic targets – six pounds one week, eight the next – and would get really excited when he jumped on the scales and found he'd achieved his goal. As time went by the weight dropped off – avoiding alcohol definitely helped in this respect – and his huge frame began to shrink before my eyes. As his clothes got baggier, his smile got wider.

'Looking great, Tyson,' I'd say, 'but I think it's time to go shopping. Your T-shirts look like tents.'

While he and I discussed his progress every day – I was keen to keep his spirits up – I also regularly checked in with Ben. I needed his reassurance that this amazing turnaround wasn't a blip, that Tyson was heading in the right direction, and that everything wasn't about to come crashing down. Ben suggested this was a slow road, not a fast track – he was still months away from regaining his fighting weight – but, crucially, his thirst for competitive sport had returned. He was in his element back at camp – skipping, sparring, shadow-boxing – and, according to Ben, this continuous activity was key.

'He has to keep training, Paris. That's the secret. He needs that routine. He needs that purpose. Without it, his mood will dip again.'

Not only was Tyson thriving in the gym, he was thriving outside it, too. Whenever he was back at the apartment, it felt like I was living with a different person. He seemed so much happier, and healthier, and I could hardly wipe the smile off my face. Our family time together was blissful. We'd walk into the hills, or stroll along the marina, often stopping off for drinks and ice creams along the way. As I pushed Valencia in her pram I'd watch the children laughing and joking with their daddy, and I'd almost have to pinch myself. Being part of a 'normal' family unit again, with Tyson on top form, felt weird but wonderful. I couldn't quite believe this was the same man who, only months previously, had preferred to get drunk in the pub with his cronies rather than have fun in the sun with his kids.

The day after we'd arrived in Marbella, Dave and Cathy had flown over to join us. They were going to stay for the entire eight weeks, in the next-door apartment. Our friends were keen to offer Tyson their moral and practical support – it was a real team effort by us all – and it was so great having them around. Sometimes, when Tyson had a break from training, he and Dave would go for long drives in the mountains and Cathy and I would head into Marbella to do some shopping or sightseeing.

Dave and Cathy kindly agreed to babysit for us, too, which enabled Tyson and me to have our first meal out in ages.

Our date nights had been non-existent since the Klitschko fight – as had romance, for that matter – and it was so nice to be together, just the two of us.

'This feels really strange,' I said to Tyson as I walked over to the car, wearing a pretty summer dress that hadn't seen the light of day for two years.

'Making up for lost time, aren't we?' He smiled. He was looking smart and handsome in a shirt and trouser outfit that, six months previously, he'd have been unable to fit into.

We headed into Puerto Banús, a coastal resort that swarmed with tourists in July and August but was lovely and quiet in the low season. We walked along the harbour, holding hands like a pair of love-struck teenagers, and found ourselves a cosy little restaurant. Over a healthy meal – low carb, of course, with bottles of water to drink, not wine – we chatted away about all sorts of things . . . with one exception. I didn't feel it was the right time or place to discuss Tyson's period of illness. There would come a day, sometime in the future, when we'd both reflect on his nightmarish two years, maybe once things had settled down and our lives were properly back on track. But Tyson had come to Marbella to recover and recuperate, and I didn't want anything to jeopardise that. There was no point in going over old ground and dredging up painful memories, which could easily trigger his anxiety and reignite his depression. So, with that in mind, I made sure we stuck to feel-good conversation topics like our family, and our future.

*   *   *

Towards the end of February we reluctantly waved goodbye to Marbella and headed back to Morecambe. We'd had a fabulous time in Spain – it had been a tonic for all of us, not least Tyson – but it was time to go home. The older children needed to return to primary school (their teachers had been great, and had appreciated our circumstances) and Tyson had some exciting work-related business in the UK to attend to. Not only had his boxing licence been reinstated – the sporting authorities had given him a clean bill of health, thank goodness – but he was about to join forces with one of the best promoters in the business, Frank Warren, to plan his boxing comeback, sometime later in the year.

During the long drive back to England there were plenty of speakerphone chats with Frank, and the Fury family, about possible dates, venues and opponents. I hadn't seen Tyson so upbeat and enthusiastic for a long time ('I feel like a fish returning to the river,' he said to one of his brothers, which made me smile). I'd never doubted his comeback – I knew he had it in him – but it was great to see the dream becoming a reality.

Tyson's comeback fight was arranged for early June – against Albanian boxer Sefer Seferi – and, much to his delight, the venue was confirmed as the Manchester Arena. It had been Tyson's long-time ambition to box professionally in his home city, and he'd been so upset when David Haye had pulled out of their scheduled fight at the same location, five years previously. He couldn't wait to use the occasion as a chance to thank the legions of devoted fans who'd supported him during his two-year absence, many of whom were based in the north.

Now Tyson had turned over a new leaf, he decided to take on a new image: the Gypsy King. In the past he'd been reluctant to embrace this particular name, questioning whether he was worthy of a title that had been given to a long line of legendary bare-knuckle fighters, including his ancestors Bartley Gorman and Uriah 'Big Just' Burton. However, once he'd been crowned world heavyweight champion, he felt he finally deserved that status on merit; he *was* the finest Gypsy fighter on Earth, when all was said and done. Tyson was very proud of his Traveller heritage – as was I, of course – and he liked the fact that, by embracing this new 'brand', he could celebrate our culture on a global stage.

Six weeks before the fight Tyson and his team set up camp in Manchester, training at ex-boxing champ Ricky Hatton's gym and staying at a nearby hotel. I'd go over to see him most weekends, with all four kids in tow, and when he had some free time we'd enjoy family meals and shopping trips together. It was during one particular visit that I uttered three little words that, over the years, he'd become quite accustomed to hearing.

'Tyson, I'm pregnant.'

While we were both chuffed to bits, this wasn't something we'd exactly planned. Valencia was still only six months old and, with Tyson being based at the moment in Manchester, the timing could have been better. In his absence, I'd taken on the lion's share of the childcare duties and the household jobs, including those that Tyson usually looked after like sorting the recycling, putting out the bins and doing the school run. I hardly had any time to rest or relax. I didn't feel resentful – I wasn't the only wife whose husband's job took him away from home – but being constantly on the go from Monday to Sunday proved to be really tough. I still found time to give Tyson his nightly morale-boosting phone call, though, once all four kids were in bed.

'So glad that training's going well,' I'd say. 'Keep up the good work, Gypsy King. I'm so proud of you.'

'Thanks for the pep talk, Paris,' he'd reply. 'Now go and put your feet up. You sound shattered.'

Sometimes people would ask me why I didn't employ any hired help – it wasn't as if we couldn't afford it – but that just wasn't the Traveller way. As proud and dedicated wives and mothers, we considered it our duty and our privilege to look after our homes and children ourselves. I was also keen to set a good example to my children. I didn't like the idea of them growing up with chefs and cleaners grafting away around us while I waltzed around all day looking glamorous. By seeing me getting stuck into all the day-to-day tasks, and by lending a hand themselves, my kids would come to realise that running a household was hard work.

Whenever I was pregnant, though, I'd gladly welcome a little help from friends and family – Mam, Cathy and Shannon often came over, which I appreciated – but I still put a shift in myself.

Just get on with it, Paris, I'd say to myself as I washed, dusted and vacuumed. I tried to take it all in my stride and be everything to everyone, like I was some kind of superwoman.

A few days before the fight, however, I found myself attending an unscheduled appointment at the antenatal clinic. I'd fallen ill at home – Mam had come over to Morecambe to watch over the children – and, just to be on the safe side, I thought I'd get myself checked out. I was a bit worried I'd overdone it with the housework, and I knew I'd not allowed myself enough downtime. I was given an early scan – I was only about seven weeks pregnant – and, much to my relief, I was informed the baby's heart was still beating and there was no immediate cause for concern. As I drove myself home from hospital I thought it best not to mention anything to Tyson. This was one of the most important fights of his career, and I didn't want to distract him in any way.

The day of the fight arrived – Saturday 9 June – and that morning I drove over to Manchester, still feeling quite unwell. Sitting on the back seat were Venezuela and Prince, who, against my better judgement, had been allowed to come and watch their dad's comeback. I'd never taken them to any of Tyson's fights before, for good reason, and during the fight build-up I'd ignored their constant pleas for ringside tickets.

I'd always insisted that live boxing matches weren't appropriate for young children, especially if it was their own father trading punches. Watching televised fights wasn't so bad, in my view, because at least there was an off button to press if things went wrong. I'd witnessed at close quarters the horrors of cuts, concussion and knockouts (usually suffered by Tyson's opponents, granted) and I felt it was my duty to shield my kids from any traumatic incidents that might leave lasting mental scars. While I had every faith in Tyson's boxing ability, he hadn't fought profession- ally for two years and anything could happen.

Venezuela and Prince were old enough to have an opin- ion, however – she was eight, he was six – and they badg- ered me constantly, even though they knew what my answer would be. Tyson reckoned I was being a proper Grinch.

'If they want to come, let them come,' he'd said. 'It's only down the road in Manchester. And I'd like them both to be there, to be honest. It'd give me a nice boost.'

'OK, just this once, but you know my thoughts on the matter,' I'd replied, resigned to the fact that Tyson had won this particular argument.

When we finally met up with Tyson at his Manchester hotel, he could sense I wasn't on top form. He told me I looked pale, and asked if I was all right – I was OK, I fibbed, just a bit under the weather – but, in reality, I was starting to feel worse. I excused myself to the bathroom and, as Tyson bounced around on the bed with the kids, with just a thin wall between us, I discovered I'd lost the baby.

I was devastated, like any woman would be in that situa- tion, but I knew I couldn't breathe a word to Tyson. With just hours to go until the fight he needed to be calm and cool-headed, and I knew for certain that this dreadful news would derail him. There was nothing to gain by telling him, I reckoned, so for the time being I'd keep it all in, let him get on with the fight, and speak to him the following day. In my mind, there was simply no other option. This comeback meant so much to him – he'd turned his life around to reach this point – and, despite my heartbreak, I felt this was the right thing to do.

I did my very best to hold it together and hide my feelings. I composed myself in the bathroom with some long, deep breaths, before emerging to tell Tyson, very calmly, that I needed to go outside.

'I've left my handbag in the car,' I said. 'I'll be back in a sec.'

'OK.' He smiled. 'I'll go and grab the kids a drink from the bar.'

I ran to the car, sat in the driver's seat, rested my head on the steering wheel and sobbed my heart out. I needed that five minutes on my own, to let my emotions flood out. Once the tears stopped rolling I stared into the rear-view mirror, dabbed my cheeks with a tissue and carefully reapplied my make-up. The next few hours were going to be as tough as hell, but my instincts told me I'd be able to battle through. My mam had brought me up to be strong, even during the most testing times – she too had experienced the trauma of baby loss – and it was with her in mind that I pulled myself together, put on my game face, and walked back into the hotel.

*　　*　　*

The Manchester Arena was packed with thousands of excited fans that afternoon, as the stage was set for the big homecoming. Two hours prior to the fight I'd taken my seat at the ringside, just a few metres away from Tyson's corner. While I still felt pretty shaken up after that morning's events, I vowed to concentrate on the fight and not let myself get distracted, not least by my two restless and fidgety children. Prince and Venezuela were sitting either side of me and spent most of the build-up complaining about the noise, begging me for snacks and drinks, playing on my phone or asking to go for a pee.

When the stadium lights went low, however, and Tyson's entrance music started playing, their little eyes widened and they became glued to their seats. Dressed in a black robe with a gold 'Gypsy King' logo on the back, he bobbed and weaved his way through the crowd, lip-synching to a tongue-in-cheek mixtape that comprised Eminem's 'Guess who's back, back again . . .' rap, Afroman's 'Because I Got High' and Mark Morrison's 'Return of the Mack'. And, as Tyson joined his opponent in the ring, he briefly turned round to give me and the kids a wink and a smile. He looked so chilled and relaxed, almost as if he'd never been away.

The music faded, the lights went up, and the Master of Ceremonies grabbed the microphone.

'In the blue corner, weighing in at nineteen stone ten pounds, hailing from right here in Manchester, England . . . *TYSON FURY . . .*'

The Arena erupted. There was so much love and affection for their home-town hero, and I knew how happy that would have made Tyson feel. It also made me realise how much I'd missed boxing myself. The sport had played a huge part in my life over the years, so being detached from that cycle of chaos and craziness had felt really strange. Boxing had been my 'normal' ever since I'd got together with Tyson, and it felt so great to be involved again.

The bout itself was an anticlimax – Seferi didn't put up much of a fight, and his camp threw in the towel after just four rounds – but to me, what mattered most was the significance of the occasion. Against all odds Tyson had staged a remarkable turnaround, and I don't think I'd ever felt so proud of him.

As Tyson celebrated in the ring I put my troubles on the back burner and put my arms round my children.

'Daddy's back,' I said, pulling them in close.

CHAPTER SEVEN

CALIFORNIA DREAMING

AFTER A DARK cloud, there sometimes comes a beautiful rainbow. Within weeks of suffering my miscarriage I discovered I was pregnant again and, following a very unhappy time in my life, I found myself able to smile once more. Telling Tyson about our baby loss, shortly after his fight in Manchester, had been horrendous. His long-awaited comeback had been such a momentous occasion, but I'd been unable to keep my sad secret any longer. I'd broken the news to Tyson in the dressing room while he'd been soaking up his victory; it was the last thing he'd expected to hear.

'You should have told me this morning,' he said, burying his face in his towel. 'You shouldn't have had to cope alone.'

'Tyson, there was no point,' I explained. 'It wouldn't have changed anything. And I didn't want you going into an important fight with that playing on your mind.'

We hugged each other and had a good cry, telling each other we'd get through this awful situation together, just like we'd done before. I had been Tyson's rock in the past and, in my time of need, I knew he'd be mine.

Now that I was expecting again, however, I decided to take better care of myself and slow my pace of life right down. Doctors had told me not to blame myself for the miscarriage – it would have happened anyway, they reckoned – but I was still concerned I'd overdone things in those vital early weeks. I'd spent too much time and energy worrying about the children, and the housework, and Tyson's comeback, when I really should have taken my foot off the gas and allowed myself more rest and relaxation. Like many busy mums, I'd become used to putting others before me, but I now realised there were limits. For the duration of this pregnancy, I'd treat myself with more kindness, and would accept generous offers of help from family and friends.

Tyson helped me in a practical sense, too. Since emerging from the depths of depression he'd returned to being a helpful husband and hands-on father, willingly assisting me with the housework (he was a whizz with a vacuum) and happily minding the children.

'No, Paris, don't even think about picking Valencia up,' he'd say, wagging his finger. 'Let me do that.'

It was lovely to see Tyson becoming a fully-functioning member of the family again. After the Manchester fight, and after losing our baby, I'd been really concerned his mood might dip – as it had done following previous bouts – yet throughout the summer he'd managed to stay relatively level-headed. He had occasional ups and downs, like most people do, but certainly nothing like the dark days of old.

Tyson's second comeback fight, against Italian boxer

Francesco Pianeta, took place at Belfast's Windsor Park stadium in August 2018. Despite it pouring with rain, the atmosphere was incredible. Belfast is a city with a great boxing tradition, and Tyson's supporters turned up in their droves; he had plenty of family connections in Northern Ireland and felt very much at home.

Among the 25,000-strong crowd was US boxer Deontay Wilder, the WBC (World Boxing Council) heavyweight champion. 'The Bronze Bomber' had built up a fearsome reputation – he was undefeated in forty fights, with thirty-nine knockouts – and, according to many, had the hardest punch in boxing. Tyson was being touted as a possible challenger to his world title belt – subject to a victory over Pianeta – and Wilder had flown to Belfast to check out the competition. When word got out the American was in attendance, Tyson asked the organisers to change his entrance music to Lynyrd Skynyrd's 'Sweet Home Alabama', in a cheeky nod to Wilder's home state.

'Top trolling, there,' laughed Tyson's brother Hughie, who'd taken his seat beside me, as per usual, with Shane to my left. Sitting next to my brothers-in-law had become a superstition as well as a comfort throughout Tyson's professional career. He'd never lost while the three of us had sat in our little row – for that reason, we never changed our ritual – and we heavily relied on each other for moral support. The brothers behaved very differently during fights, though. Hughie, like me, was a nervous wreck who panicked too much, whereas Shane was far more relaxed and focused. He had this big, booming voice, too, so I'd often ask him to yell stuff up to Tyson, because my shouts usually got drowned out. Tyson says he can always hear his brother's foghorn voice in the crowd, even in a stadium of 50,000 people.

'Tell him to move in,' I'd say, giving Shane a nudge. 'Tell him *now* . . .'

'MOVE IN, TYSON . . . *MOVE IN* . . .' he'd bellow on my behalf.

Fortunately, the Belfast bout was pretty straightforward, and I had no need to give Shane a prod. Tyson had trained really hard and was in great shape – he'd weighed in at under nineteen stone – and he easily beat Pianeta on points. It was the post-fight shenanigans that hogged the following day's headlines, though. Wilder had brought his title belt to Windsor Park – presumably for some bragging rights – and Tyson had jokingly snatched it away and slung it across his shoulder before parading it around the ring. The pair had then squared up for some trash talk, with Wilder proclaiming their super-fight was well and truly on, and Tyson threatening to knock him out if that was the case. The crowd loved it, as did the media.

The respective boxing promoters got to work, and a date was finally set for a pay-per-view Fury–Wilder showdown: Saturday 1 December at Los Angeles' Staples Center. Not everybody was thrilled about it, though. There were some boxing experts (including Tyson's father) who reckoned this bout had been arranged prematurely, and might be a bridge too far for Tyson. Many questioned the calibre of his opponents in Manchester and Belfast (Seferi and Pianeta weren't in the same league as

Wilder, admittedly) and others suggested he was too ring-rusty to tackle such a big fight. But Tyson and his team were confident that, with the right preparation and training, he'd have a decent chance of beating Wilder and reclaiming his heavyweight crown.

On the day of the announcement I flicked through my kitchen calendar and worked out that, at the beginning of December, I'd be seven months pregnant. I made a mental note to have a chat with my GP about the chances of me flying to LA, because I was desperate to be there for Tyson. He'd be facing one of the most dangerous boxers on the planet – someone who knocked out opponents for fun – and I wanted to be there in person, not watching it on telly. If anything went wrong, I needed to be at Tyson's side, not across the ocean.

Tyson and I were 5,000 miles apart when we celebrated our tenth wedding anniversary. He was in California, holed up in the renowned Big Bear training camp, and I was in Lancashire, home alone with four kids. Before the confirmation of the Wilder fight, though, my husband had been planning a massive anniversary party for our friends and family. There'd even been talk of one of Tyson's favourite singers, Tom Jones, making a special guest appearance (one of the perks of being well-known is having access to a network of contacts in the showbiz circuit, who can make these things happen). Our big celebration had to be shelved, however, when the fight date was set and the contract was signed.

'Paris, you must be gutted it's not going ahead,' said a pal of mine, but to be honest, I wasn't that upset. I'd never been a party person – a nice meal for two would have been enough for me – and a big bash was more Tyson's scene than mine. Also – and this may be an unpopular opinion – I've always found wedding anniversaries to be overrated. They're not a big deal to me. I love Tyson to bits, and I'm so proud to be his wife, but I see our anniversary as just another date in the diary that comes and goes; a reminder that another year has been notched up. Tyson has come to realise I'm perfectly happy with a greetings card, a bunch of flowers and a big kiss, which is exactly what he sent me all the way from LA (minus the kiss, sadly).

Some of my indifference no doubt stems from the fact that, throughout our marriage, Tyson has missed so many important events – Venezuela's birth, for starters, and lots of family weddings – and I've learned to accept it as part and parcel of life with a busy boxer. That being said, one occasion remains totally sacred. Our family has never been apart at Christmas – Tyson just won't allow that to happen, wherever he is in the world – and there have been times when I've packed a family-sized suitcase and jetted out to spend the festive season with him at a training camp in Miami or Las Vegas.

I flew over to Los Angeles four days before the Wilder fight. My doctor had given me the all-clear on condition that I took things gently on the plane and did my circulation-boosting exercises. I left the children at home in Morecambe, in the loving care of their Granny Lynda. The fact she adored spending time with her grandchildren, and vice versa, made my goodbyes so much easier. Thinking about it, I honestly don't know how I'd have managed without Mam's help over the years. I certainly wouldn't have been able to travel the world to watch Tyson fight, that's for sure. She is such an amazing mother and grandmother. She will do anything for my kids – she shows them the same devotion she showed me as a child – and I'm pretty sure she'd take two or three of them back home with her if she could.

'Oh my God, Paris, your mam's *so* good with your little ones,' my friends will often say, as they watch her playing with them in the garden.

'I know,' I'll say, smiling. 'I'm so lucky to have her.'

It was fabulous to hook up with Tyson in LA. We hadn't seen each other for nearly two months – in that time, my baby bump had doubled in size – and he'd missed me as much as I'd missed him. The training camp had gone well, he reckoned (half of it had been spent at altitude at Big Bear, and the other half in the city) and he was raring to go and ready for the challenge.

However, as the fight night loomed closer my anxiety levels skyrocketed, more so than any other fight that had gone before it. While I had every faith in my husband's confidence and ability – I only needed to cast my mind back to what he'd achieved in the Klitschko fight – I couldn't rid myself of a sick feeling in the pit of my stomach. I was so worried this head-to-head was too much, too soon and that, by stepping into the ring to fight Wilder, Tyson was putting his health at serious risk. Just one mega-punch could easily knock him unconscious, cause him brain damage or, God help us, endanger his life.

Earlier that year, a professional boxer had tragically died from a knockout blow. This awful news had shocked me to the core, and had hammered home how perilous this sport could be. While I chose not to discuss my innermost fears with Tyson – I didn't want to dampen his spirits – I'm pretty sure he could sense my nervousness.

Tyson's father – whose criminal record had prevented him from getting a US visa and travelling to LA – had similar fears and reservations. Unlike me, though, John made his feelings quite clear. He thought his son and his entourage were making a catastrophic mistake in fighting Wilder so soon. In fact, he was so angry and upset he refused to speak to Tyson for weeks, only breaking his silence to wish him good luck in a phone call from Manchester. While this sad situation had come as a blow to Tyson – he worshipped his dad, and had always valued his advice – it didn't dent his confidence. He was still sure he could win.

Fight night finally arrived and, two hours before the main event, Shane, Hughie and I took our ringside seats at the Staples Center. We were so nervous we could hardly speak or think straight; even Shane seemed more jumpy and jittery than usual. We knew full well this was the riskiest fight of Tyson's career to date, and we'd no idea what lay in store for him. I was past caring whether he won or lost; I just wanted him to survive. I needed this fight over and done with, so we could jump onto a plane and fly straight back home.

Unlike his keyed-up family, Tyson appeared calm and composed when he climbed through the ropes to face his opponent. Other boxers might have been intimidated by a sinister-looking Deontay Wilder, sporting a gold crown, mask and gloves, but Tyson – dressed in a plain black Gypsy King T-shirt – seemed totally unruffled.

'Live from Los Angeles ... it's SHOWTIME!' yelled the Master of Ceremonies. No doubt millions of people around the world were glued to their TVs with their beer and popcorn, gearing up to watch these two warriors slug it out. Funnily enough, I wasn't in the mood to be entertained. I just felt like throwing up.

The first-round bell rang, and I can only describe what followed as thirty-six minutes of sheer hell. This was despite the fact that, as far as I could tell, Tyson was out-boxing his opponent; by putting him under pressure, and landing some decent shots, he was effectively suppressing Wilder's punch-power. Those who had openly questioned the Gypsy King's fitness and stamina (and there'd been many) would have been eating their words as a lean-and-mean-looking Tyson danced around the ring, fully focused on the task in hand.

Wilder had some good spells of activity, too, even managing to knock Tyson down in the ninth round; he didn't seem badly hurt, thank God, and scrambled to his feet straight away. As each round progressed, Tyson remained in control. Shane said he was giving Wilder a boxing lesson in his own backyard. This fight was going better than Team Fury could ever have imagined.

But events soon took a dramatic turn. Just thirty seconds into the final round, Wilder unleashed a powerful right-hand punch, swiftly followed by another left-hander, which smashed into Tyson's jaw and caused him to crash to the floor. He lay flat on his back, completely still. You could hear the whole crowd gasp. The referee dashed over and began the count: *one, two, three . . .*

I felt myself crumble. I heard myself scream. My worst fear seemed to have been realised, and for a moment I genuinely thought Tyson was dead. My immediate impulse was to clamber over the barrier and go to his aid but, suddenly remembering I was seven months pregnant, I yelled at Shane to do it instead. But just as I gave my brother-in-law a frantic shove towards the ring, the unthinkable happened.

. . . four, five, six . . .

Halfway through the countdown, Tyson pulled himself up from the canvas. He shook himself down, bounced on his tiptoes, raised his gloves to his face and squared up to Wilder, as if the knockdown had never happened. I could hardly believe my eyes. I'd attended countless fights in my life, yet this was the most incredible thing I'd ever seen in a boxing ring. Wilder must have wondered what the hell was going on. He might have thought it was game over; Tyson certainly didn't.

But there were still two minutes remaining, and I was terrified that, having smelled blood, Wilder would try to finish off the job good and proper by causing some serious damage to Tyson. From my ringside seat I begged my husband to act sensibly and protect himself.

'Guard up!' I kept shouting, as loudly as I could. '*GUARD UP!*'

But Tyson was having none of it. His fighting instincts told him to go on the attack and dominate the rest of the round. That final two minutes felt like two hours. It was torture. I winced every time Tyson advanced towards Wilder and swung a punch, and I willed the final bell to ring. When it did, the relief washed over me like a tidal wave. The fight was over, thank God, and my husband was still standing. More than that, in fact. He was parading around the ring with his arms aloft, justifiably soaking up the adulation from a crowd who'd never witnessed a comeback like it.

'Did that really just happen?' I said to Hughie, who seemed as astonished as me.

'Crazy, Paris. Absolutely crazy . . .'

Although the result wasn't my prime concern, it was a huge let-down when it came. I think everyone in the Staples Center expected Tyson to be crowned the winner – in spite of the knockdowns, he'd controlled the fight – but the MC announced it as a draw. There was a great deal of anger and confusion in the dressing room afterwards. No one could understand the logic behind the verdict; most of us reckoned it was a travesty, and Tyson had been robbed of a rightful victory. The only person who accepted the result was the man himself; I couldn't help but admire his chilled-out attitude.

'It is what it is,' he said, trying to calm the mood. 'Yes, of course I think I won the fight, but what's the use getting all wound up? There's nothing we can do about it. Bring on the rematch.'

Later that evening, when Tyson and I returned to our hotel room, all the emotions I'd kept hidden for days spilled out. I cleaned off my make-up, unpeeled my false nails, lay down on the bed and sobbed my heart out. As Tyson cradled me in a big hug, I told him I never, ever wanted to live through that experience again. The fight had turned a tough cookie like me into a nervous wreck, and the fear of him getting injured – or worse – had been hard to handle, especially in my condition. At one stage I even demanded he quit boxing for good, although, deep down, I knew that wouldn't happen any time soon. Tyson still had unfinished business. I just wanted him to do it as safely as possible, for his sake, and for his family's sake.

During the lead-up to the Wilder fight, while doing the usual media rounds, Tyson had started to discuss his mental health issues in great depth. He felt instinctively it was the right time to open up and tell the world what he'd gone through. Since that fateful Halloween night, six months earlier, he'd given himself time to process his period of severe depression and, slowly but surely, he'd built up the strength and confidence to talk about it publicly. I thought this was a very brave and admirable thing to do. He told me he wanted to use his fame to help raise awareness and reduce the stigma of depressive illness, and to reassure fellow sufferers they weren't alone.

'I hate the thought of anybody else going through all that pain, Paris, and if I can help just one person, then I'll be happy.'

'I'm right behind you, Tyson.'

Me, Shane and Hughie had been with Tyson in a Los Angeles press briefing room, just before the fight, when he'd spoken publicly about his illness for the first time, to a group of boxing reporters. He'd spoken straight from the heart, describing with brutal honesty how he'd spiralled into depression, lost his way in life and contemplated suicide.

Even though I'd lived through this whole experience with him – and definitely recognised the 'old Tyson' he was referring to – seeing him talk so beautifully, and with such courage, was very, very moving. I just about managed to keep it together, but his brothers were in tears, and some of the reporters were, too. At one point Hughie had to leave the room because he was so overwhelmed with emotion; hearing the true extent of Tyson's suffering was almost too much for him to bear. He'd not realised at the time how much pain Tyson had been in.

As Tyson opened up more often, the response was overwhelmingly positive – the sports media were particularly sympathetic – and, in the spring and summer of 2019,

Tyson decided he wanted to connect more directly with the public. He joined forces with an events company and toured venues and theatres around the UK, appearing in front of big audiences to talk about the highs and lows of his professional and personal life so far, from lifting his title belt in Düsseldorf to nearly driving into a bridge in Lancaster. He was so keen to spread the message that anyone, regardless of status or background, could experience low mood and low self-esteem – even the heavyweight champion of the world – but that it was also possible to get your life back on track.

'First and foremost, get yourself to your GP,' was his advice to anyone struggling with poor mental health.

Being so honest about his experiences with depression had a big effect on his audience, and Tyson would tell me how he'd look into the auditorium and see grown men in floods of tears. I was struck too that, by laying his life bare, he was also able to be more honest with himself, and more kind. Being a champion boxer didn't mean he had to be a superhero. Beneath his macho man, alpha-male exterior, he was revealing a human being with human vulnerabilities.

'I'm so proud of him for doing this,' I remember saying to Montana as we chatted on the phone. My sister and I were still very close, although we didn't see each other as often as we liked because she lived over in Lincolnshire with her husband and kids.

'You're right to be proud,' she replied. 'It takes guts to speak so honestly to a roomful of strangers. And it's great that people are seeing a side to him that's not usually on show.'

Montana was spot on. Everybody knew Tyson Fury was a brilliant sportsman, but not everybody knew Tyson Fury as a decent, caring family man; a loving husband, brother, son and father. As I often told him, he was my gentle giant.

Following a very easy and enjoyable pregnancy, our third son – Prince Adonis Amaziah – was born in February 2019 at Royal Lancaster Infirmary. When we'd discovered I was expecting a boy, at the twenty-week scan, Tyson and I had both agreed on Amaziah as a middle name – it means 'strength of the Lord' in Hebrew – but for a while we couldn't make our minds up about a Christian name to follow Prince. Not long after the Wilder fight, however, we chose Adonis. It was already on my shortlist – I liked the idea of the Greek god of beauty – but Tyson also had his own reasons. The same night Tyson had faced Wilder, a boxer called Adonis Stevenson had fought in Quebec City but had suffered a knockout blow and sadly slipped into a coma. He'd later go on to make a recovery, thankfully, but Tyson felt that, by honouring his name in this way, he'd be paying his own little homage to a very brave fighter.

The spring and summer of 2019 was a blissfully happy time for me and Tyson. He was firmly back on track, both in and out of the ring, and I was enjoying motherhood like never before. Carrying, birthing and raising children now felt like second nature to me – I'd been pregnant for nearly half of our marriage – and Tyson and I saw each of our five beautiful children as a gift from God. Big families were in my bloodline, of course – my Granny Mary had raised eight kids – and I'd always yearned for a houseful of children. As our brood grew from four to five – with three of them in nappies – I felt totally blessed that my dreams had come true. I'd often joke that I was trying to keep up with Morecambe's famous Radford family, who, at the time of Adonis' birth, had twenty children in their household.

As time's gone by, it's been nice seeing our kids' personalities starting to emerge. Our eldest, Venezuela, is a very kind and respectful girl who's taken on the 'big sister' role beautifully, always keeping an eye on the little ones and keeping them in check. She's independent and self-sufficient, a bit like me, and she's sporty and athletic, just like Tyson; in fact, they'll often go for runs together. Prince John James is the most laid-back of all our children. He lives life at half-speed, loves lazing around the house and – as his head is often in the clouds – he needs to be told something five times before it registers. But he's very loving, a real puppy-dog, and is often the first to ask me for a cuddle.

Prince Tyson, however, couldn't be more different. I don't know whether it's middle-child syndrome, whereby he has to shout the loudest for attention, but he's the noisiest and naughtiest of the lot. We didn't know what had hit us when he was born – he rarely slept, and he constantly cried – and he was walking at ten months, and running at eleven (and hasn't stopped since). While he's a handful, and that's putting it mildly, Tyson's also a really funny kid who often makes us cry with laughter.

Some of his cheekiness has definitely rubbed off on younger sister, Valencia, who has her wild moments, but who's also very sweet and affectionate; she's always hugging and petting her cuddly toys, and she's the sort of girl who'd give you her last Rolo. Prince Adonis is our quietest child – he's quite thoughtful and considerate and, of the five, is probably most similar to his dad in personality. But when he loses his temper – if someone pinches his toys, or switches off his favourite TV show – we all know about it. It's like a volcano erupting.

Coping with five kids has certainly had its challenges but, to be honest, by the time our third came along – Tyson junior – I felt I'd got motherhood down to a fine art. As my self-confidence increased each baby-stage became more familiar, and things just fell into place. I changed their nappies, made up bottles, gave them baths and strapped them into our family-sized Transit van like I was on autopilot.

I'm by no means the perfect parent – I don't think such a thing exists – but years of practice and experience has taught me what works best for the Fury family. First and foremost, I need to be as organised as possible. Getting all the kids washed, dressed and fed each morning, for instance, has to be approached like a military operation. This means ensuring all their clothes and uniforms are washed, ironed and folded beforehand – I try to avoid last-minute scrabbling around in laundry baskets – and keeping my food cupboards and fridge-freezer well stocked up so I can quickly rustle up their meals, and not flap around looking for things for them to eat.

Doing my best to stick to a daily routine helps, too, and during the week I try to keep mealtimes, bathtimes and bedtimes as regular as possible. These rules fall by the wayside at weekends and in school holidays, of course, but I'm fine with that; things can be a little more free-and-easy then, and we can all chill out a bit more. We might drive out to the countryside for an afternoon or, if the weather's good, have a barbecue in the garden.

Being married to a sportsman whose schedule can change from hour to hour means I've got to be pretty flexible and adaptable, too. Me and the kids might be in London, doing a bit of sightseeing while Tyson has some business to attend to, and he'll announce a sudden change in schedule.

'Something's cropped up, Paris. I need a few more hours here. We'll have to stay overnight.'

'That's fine, I'll work it,' I'll say, before gathering up the kids and heading to the supermarket to buy some cheapo pyjamas and some travel-size toiletries, while Tyson sorts a couple of family rooms in a hotel.

I've never let the children hold me back and I've always had a can-do mindset, even with five of them in tow. I rarely use them as an excuse to duck out of things, whether it's a last-minute holiday abroad (Tyson's been known to spring this on me with a day to spare) or a spur-of-the-moment family gathering. I just roll with it. I like being constantly on the go. It must be my Traveller spirit.

Essential to the smooth(ish) running of our household is a real 'muck-in' attitude, too, which is definitely a throwback to my own upbringing. Back at Tilts Farm, sons and daughters always lightened their parents' load by doing various chores and I'm happy to carry on this tradition. Now they're old enough, Prince and Venezuela have their own jobs, whether it's cleaning the windows, vacuuming the carpet or stacking the dishwasher. The little ones get involved, too – start 'em young, I say – and Baby Tyson often helps me to unload the tumble dryer and fold the family underwear. Left to my own devices with a Vileda mop or a vacuum cleaner, I'd probably do these jobs in half the time, but it's the principle that matters. I think it's really important my children learn life skills; I don't want them growing up assuming everything gets done for them. Occasionally they'll moan and groan when I crack the whip, though.

'Aw, Mam, do I have to clean the bathroom?'

'Yes, you do, Prince. Or d'you want your poor mother to do everything?'

I have Tyson's full support. He agrees our children should pull their weight – 'no one gets a free ride,' he'll say – and everyone in the Fury family has their own part to play. To give him his due, when Tyson's not away at a training camp he's a great help around the house. He hates mess and clutter – not uncommon for someone with OCD – so can often be found tidying up or going to the tip. He's brilliant when it comes to looking after the kids, too, and is more than capable of getting them washed, dressed and fed before taking them to school or nursery. To make our lives easier, Tyson and I often split the childcare, so he might take Prince and Venezuela to visit his mam in Manchester while I take the little ones to the park.

I do try my best as a mother, but things don't always run smoothly, and I don't get it right all the time. Sometimes Fury Towers can be complete pandemonium, with a baby bawling in one room, and a toddler tantrumming in the other, and I'll be troubleshooting and firefighting all over the place. Having a big family can come in handy, though, because the older kids will often help me with the younger kids.

'Can you play with Valencia and Adonis in the garden while I do the tea?' I'll ask Prince and Venezuela, who'll happily oblige.

While I try to set clear boundaries for the children – there are many things I won't tolerate, like bad language or bad manners – sometimes they'll overstep the mark and I'll find myself losing my rag. Like most parents, I have my tipping point and will often blow my top. I'm probably stricter with the kids than Tyson (they definitely get away with more when he's around) but I put that down to his long absences from home. Whenever he returns from a two-month training camp he's overjoyed to see the kids – he misses them so much – and the last thing he wants to do is give them a good telling-off.

Being a mother is the best job in the world, in my opinion, but it can often seem like the hardest job in the world. Days can pass when I don't get a single minute to myself (I can be preparing bottles for the baby one minute, and potty training a toddler the next) but I've just learned to accept that it's par for the course. If I'd wanted the life of Riley I wouldn't have chosen to have a big bunch of kids. Sometimes all the mayhem gets too much for my eldest – 'Oh, I'm sick of these kids . . .' Venezuela will say, when the noise levels hit the roof – but then I tell her how much she'll appreciate her younger brothers and sisters in a few years' time. The age gaps won't seem so wide, and she'll suddenly find she has a lot more in common with them.

But along with all the chaos and commotion there's also lots of fun and laughter – I still say there's nothing nicer than the sound of a child giggling – and ours is a home full of love and affection.

In the summer of 2019 we arranged for all five kids to be christened together. We'd planned to do this as each child arrived, but Tyson's busy schedule meant we'd never quite got round to it, so we decided to do it in one go. We organised the church (St Mary's RC, not far from our house), invited friends and family, and reserved a room in a local restaurant for a buffet after the ceremony.

'So how many would you like to book for, Mrs Fury, and are there any dietary requirements?' I was asked.

'It could be anything between eighty and a hundred and fifty, so just put loads of chairs out,' I answered. 'And as for food, a massive selection of everything will do just fine, thanks.'

I had to explain that, when it came to special occasions, we Travellers didn't do specifics. I had no idea how many guests would turn up on the day – you could invite an aunt, who'd then arrive with four cousins in tow – but as long as there were enough chairs, and plenty of food and drink, you'd know everyone would be happy.

It was a beautiful christening. It meant a lot for Tyson and me to welcome the children into the Catholic faith, and it was lovely to see the church packed to the rafters with our family and friends (there must have been two hundred there in the end, who all managed to squeeze into the restaurant afterwards). The five kids were all dressed up in their Sunday best – smart suits for the boys, pretty dresses for the girls – and they were all on their very best behaviour as they were individually baptised by the priest.

Things didn't go entirely to plan, though. Baby Tyson was quite poorly on the day and, while we were all stood at the front of the church, listening to the sermon, he started to retch really badly. I knew he was about to puke up so I quickly steered him to one side of the church, yanking a muslin square off my sister as I did so. I chucked the cloth in front of Baby Tyson, just in time for him to throw up all over it. It wasn't just my husband who had impeccable timing.

Oh, the joys of motherhood, I thought, as I wiped him up and calmed him down.

Nursemaid is just another part of the 'Mam' job description, of course, along with cook, nanny, cleaner, teacher, taxi driver and so on. But would I have it any other way? Not a chance.

In June 2019 I swapped the Lancashire coast for the Nevada desert, flying over to Las Vegas to watch the next fight in my husband's busy boxing calendar. If he was to earn his much-wanted rematch against Deontay Wilder he needed a couple more wins under his belt, and a bout was lined up with undefeated German Tom Schwarz at the MGM Grand, one of the world's most famous boxing venues.

By now Tyson had signed a new, five-match agreement with US network ESPN. It was a big deal for us in so many ways, as the amount of money on the table would safeguard our family's future. Although I wasn't directly involved in Tyson's business affairs, we always discussed any new developments together (Tyson valued my opinion, which I was always very happy to give) and this ESPN offer was one he simply couldn't refuse. Personal wealth was never my husband's main driver – mine neither – but long-term financial security gave his risky line of work a little more worth and meaning.

Receiving this payout didn't change us as people, either. There may have been a few extra zeros on our bank balance, and a few more investments in our portfolio, but I felt we were still the same old Furys, with our feet still firmly on the ground. While the ESPN deal allowed us to splash out on a few luxury items – high-performance cars, designer clothes, and a beautifully renovated traditional Gypsy caravan for our back garden – we avoided spending cash like there was no tomorrow. We'd both been brought up by our parents to appreciate the value of money, and to use it wisely. We saw no reason to stop shopping in Asda and Home Bargains, and we had no immediate plans to swap our family home – which we loved, despite the increasing lack of space – for a mansion house.

Tyson had spent nearly two months in a training camp prior to the Schwarz fight, having based himself in a nearby villa along with his team. When I arrived in Las Vegas, just before the big day, I was dying to see him again. I was also looking forward to exploring the city where Mam had spent her teenage years; when I was a young girl she'd told me so many stories about her life in Vegas – the Elvis concerts, the Liberace palm readings – and I couldn't wait to see the place for myself.

We spent our first night out at a downtown hotel that boasted amazing views across the famous Strip. There was always a romantic 'first date' vibe when we hadn't seen each other for a while and, as we chatted away in the restaurant, we held hands across the table like a courting couple. He was desperate to know how the children were getting on – he always missed them like crazy – and, over dinner, I scrolled through hundreds of photos on my phone, including a very chubby Adonis wearing a mini Gypsy King outfit.

'Ah, I can't believe how much he's grown,' he said.

'I know. You'll hardly recognise him when you get back.' I smiled.

Love's young dream wasn't to last, though. The following morning, in the Team Fury villa, I found myself pulling on a pair of Marigolds to tackle a sink piled high with dirty dishes. When I'd first walked into the kitchen I'd been horrified by the mess I'd encountered – every surface was lined with grimy plates, pans and cutlery – and I'd felt compelled to clear it up straight away.

'What on earth are you playing at?' I yelled at Tyson as I stared at all the clutter. 'You're an elite athlete! You've got a huge fight coming up! You're going to catch something!'

'We've been so busy these past few days, Paris,' he replied, a little guiltily. 'We've hardly had time to tidy up after ourselves.'

So I became the resident cleaner and housemaid for the rest of my stay – it was like being home from home – but one afternoon I did manage to escape my kitchen duties to take a tour around Las Vegas. If I'm honest, I was left feeling a little disappointed. Thanks to Mam's stories I'd visualised a magical, fairy-tale city, but it was all too brash for me. Gambling and partying weren't really my scene. Some of the hotels on the Strip were stunning – and it was great to see Tyson's face staring down at me from enormous billboards – but from what I could see, Las Vegas was more like Blackpool with bells on.

On the day of the fight, once I'd had a good soak in the bath to calm my nerves, I began to get my outfit ready. Buying the right dress for the occasion was important to me, but it was never an obsession. The way I saw it, it was Tyson's moment in the spotlight, not mine. I was there in a supporting role, not a starring one. What mattered most to me was looking presentable as well as feeling comfortable. I did a lot of bouncing up and down when I watched Tyson box – sometimes I'd even climb onto my seat to get a better view – so each outfit had to pass a durability and dignity test. I couldn't have it ripping up the seam or riding up my backside.

More often than not I bought my dresses on the high street – I'd often spend less than a hundred quid – but for Fury v Schwarz, I thought I'd treat myself to an off-the-peg designer number. I was off to the MGM Grand, after all – one of boxing's spiritual homes – so I thought I should make a special effort. A few weeks before I was due to fly out, I took Mam and Montana into Manchester for a shopping trip and headed straight for Harvey Nichols.

'For once, I'm not going to think twice about the price tag,' I said.

'And rightly so,' said Mam. 'If you can't get dressed up in Las Vegas, you never will.'

I tried on outfit after outfit – from long evening gowns to short cocktail dresses – and none of them looked right. So I looked around Selfridges, too, and I didn't fancy anything there, either. All these designer pieces cost two grand, maybe three – seriously daft money for a dress I might wear only once – yet nothing suited me. So back to the high street I went. While browsing in Debenhams I made a beeline for a baby-pink Coast minidress with an ostrich-feather neckline. I tried it on in the changing room and instantly fell in love with it. The dress was perfect, as was its price tag: just £120. Tyson's pay cheques may have become larger, but I still liked getting my value for money.

Tyson's own fight-night costume was a little more outlandish. With James Brown's 'Living in America' blaring out through the speakers, he entered the arena for his Las Vegas debut dressed like *Rocky*'s Apollo Creed, top to toe in Uncle Sam-style stars and stripes. The US public had taken Tyson to their hearts – as had the country's media, who loved his zero-to-hero story – and it was his way of showing his appreciation. He was also aware that, in the entertainment capital of the world, you were expected to put on a show. And no one liked putting on a show more than Tyson.

The fight itself was over in two rounds. Tom Schwarz was on the ropes from the get-go and Tyson's speed and strength proved too much for him. I believe it was one of the fastest victories I'd ever seen and, thank God, it came as a total contrast to the trauma of the Deontay Wilder fight. As I joined Tyson in the ring afterwards, wearing my new pink dress, he sang Aerosmith's 'Don't Want to Miss a Thing' to me, just like he'd done following the Klitschko fight. It was a highly symbolic moment. Two years earlier, when our lives had been in turmoil, I'd prayed that, one day, Tyson would serenade me again. That moment had finally arrived, and it felt wonderful.

*   *   *

Later that year, in mid-September, I found myself in Las Vegas once again, this time to support Tyson as he prepared to fight Swedish boxer Otto Wallin. The bout took place on Mexican Independence Day – a big occasion in the border state of California – and Tyson recognised this by doing his ring-walk dressed in a wide sombrero and draped in a green, red and white poncho. Despite being very proud of his English and Irish roots, he's always felt quite comfortable embracing other nationalities. It's a nod to his Traveller heritage. Throughout history, Gypsies have roamed from country to country – being on the move is in our blood – and in many ways we feel we're citizens of the world, and don't belong to one particular place. It's this sense of inclusion that encourages Tyson to celebrate different cultures, and to fly their flag with pride.

It's only since Tyson embraced the Gypsy King label that we've realised how many of our people exist internationally. Everywhere he boxes, people from the Gypsy and Traveller community come to support him and, whenever we holiday abroad, lots of them recognise us and come over to say hello. It's been a real education for us; until Tyson's fame grew, we had no idea how widespread and varied our culture was. I'd always assumed that all Gypsies were Christians, but in recent times we have come across Jewish Gypsies from Israel and Muslim Gypsies from Egypt, whose ancestors have followed their respective faiths for hundreds of years.

The T-Mobile Arena was buzzing with fans from all over the world as Tyson made his grand Mexican-themed

A trip to Cannes in summer 2016. Tyson's smile doesn't tell the true story; he was very unwell and we had to come home early.

Prince, Venezuela and baby Tyson having fun during the 2016 Christmas holidays.

Tyson's bizarre behaviour during the Fury v Klitschko II press conference in April 2016 was incredibly worrying.

We added to our brood in December 2017 with the arrival of Valencia Amber.

Venezuela was delighted to have a little sister.

Some R&R in Marbella in January 2018. Tyson's recovery was progressing, and I could see the light at the end of the tunnel.

The moment when Tyson was knocked down by US boxer Deontay Wilder, in December 2018. For a second I thought he'd died.

Tyson mounted an amazing comeback, and the fight ended in a draw. I was so relieved to hear the final bell.

At Tyson's side during the press briefing in 2018 when he opened up publicly about his struggle with depression.

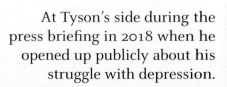

Getting ready for the children's christening. Tyson is holding baby Prince Adonis Amaziah, born February 2019. From left to right: Prince John James, Venezuela, Prince Tyson Luke, Valencia.

Looking on petrified as Tyson receives a horrific facial injury during a fight with Otto Wallin, September 2019.

Happy times with Tyson. Enjoying a sunshine break in Marbella and the surprise 30th birthday party he threw for me in Manchester in 2019.

Meeting Dwayne 'The Rock' Johnson at the Staples Center, Los Angeles, and below at Disneyworld, Florida, in 2019.

Montana and me before Tyson's fight with Tom Schwarz, in June 2019.

Tyson floors Deontay Wilder during their February 2020 rematch.

After his sensational victory over Wilder, Tyson serenaded me with a rendition of 'American Pie'.

Turning up to the *This Morning* studio in February 2020 wearing the same skirt as Holly Willoughby. Phillip Schofield found it funny too.

Baby news: Paris is pregnant

Announcing I was expecting baby number six on ITV's *Loose Women.*

Looking forward to the future.

ring-walk. Sitting alongside me was my friend Cathy, and sitting behind me was Tyson's younger brother and fellow boxer Tommy and his new girlfriend, Molly-Mae, who'd famously got together on ITV's *Love Island* reality show. Tyson had been totally supportive of his brother's decision to sign up for the programme; he thought it'd be an ideal profile-raiser that might help his career progression. I don't think he expected his fame to soar so much that people began to refer to the heavyweight champion of the world as 'Tommy Fury's brother', though. I found this really funny.

'So what's it like to have your thunder stolen by your baby brother, eh?' I said.

'I don't mind at all,' laughed Tyson. 'Fair play to him.'

Molly-Mae, who I met for the first time in Vegas, seemed really nice. She struck me as very sensible and level-headed, and seemed incredibly loved up with Tommy. We chatted about life as the partner of a fighter and, as she was relatively new to the boxing scene, I told her I was always around if she needed advice from someone who'd been there, done that, and witnessed all the highs and the lows.

Twelve minutes into Tyson's bout against Wallin, I experienced one of those lows. In the third round, the Swede aimed a left-hand punch at Tyson, which caught his eyebrow and split it open. As blood gushed from the gash, I gasped and grabbed Shane.

'It's not the eye socket is it?' I said, frightened he'd sustained one of the more serious boxing injuries.

'No, it's above it . . . but the ref could so easily stop the fight now,' he replied. If so, Wallin would win, explained Shane, because the cut was caused by his punch as opposed to an accidental clash of heads.

That would be Tyson's worst nightmare. He was so proud of his unbeaten record, and to lose to a cut – and jeopardise the Wilder rematch – would have been a bitter pill to swallow. I'd always wondered – and worried – how Tyson would react to defeat, and it looked like I was going to find out.

Watching the rest of the bout was agony, and I counted down every second until the final bell. Tyson's wound kept getting opened up – Wallin was targeting it at every opportunity – and it had to be glued up with Vaseline between each round. But despite his vision being impaired by the constant trickle of blood, Tyson soldiered on and eventually won on points; thank heavens both the doctor and the referee had decided not to stop the fight.

There was no time for a victory parade. Tyson needed to get to hospital, and quick. Arena staff ushered us straight out of the back entrance, where an ambulance, with its blue lights flashing, waited to whisk us to the nearest emergency room. There, Tyson was told that, due to the depth of the cut and the underlying muscle tear, he was going to need plastic surgery. The specialist had to be called in from home (I'd put my foot down and demanded the best plastic surgeon in the business) and the operation was performed in the early hours. The wound needed a total of forty-seven internal and external stitches.

The following morning was rough. I felt totally exhausted – I'd not slept a wink – and I was still feeling dazed after the previous night's events. Tyson, on the other hand, was remarkably cheerful, joking with Ben and the team about his English stiff upper lip and lifting his shades to show off his battle scar. I was glad to see him so upbeat – in past times, he might not have coped so well with such a setback – but my mood simply didn't echo his. I just wanted to fly back home to the UK and hug my babies. It turned out Mam had watched the whole fight with our three eldest – they'd begged to be allowed to stay up late – and, although Granny would have comforted them, I knew the gruesome images of their dad's injury would have really upset them.

Following a champagne breakfast with Team Fury at a nearby casino, I returned to the villa to pack our suitcases. I'd done my duty in Vegas, and now my children needed me in Morecambe. I could hardly wait to see them again.

CHAPTER EIGHT

IN THE SPOTLIGHT

WHEN I FIRST met Tyson, in my mid-teens, I couldn't have known how famous he'd become, and how much our lives would change. Ours has been an extraordinary journey – one that's sometimes been tough to navigate – but I'm glad that, through it all, we've both stayed level-headed and have stuck to our values and priorities.

Tyson has never been your typical celebrity. His huge boxing success may have raised his public profile, but – unless he has a fight to promote – he prefers to avoid the limelight. It speaks volumes that he chooses to base himself in Morecambe, which, while we love it, isn't the most glamorous place to live. He hardly has any famous friends – he surrounds himself with close family, and a handful of pals he's known and trusted for ages – and, over the years, he's learned to spot (and shun) the freeloaders and the parasites. He doesn't give them the time of day.

Tyson has turned down countless opportunities to appear on game shows and reality shows, too, and has even declined major TV and movie roles. While he's still enjoying his boxing, he doesn't want or need the additional exposure. The only entertaining he's keen to do is in the ring, by winning fights and gaining titles. As he's said himself, 'Fame can come and go, but achievement lasts forever.'

We've never been especially drawn to the celebrity bandwagon. But, back in the early days of Tyson's professional career, not long after our wedding, his promoters had encouraged him to try to get some more media exposure. It would be in his interest, he was told, because the more prominent the fighter, the more match tickets were sold, and the more money was earned. Tyson was put in touch with a high-profile, London-based PR firm who added him to their client list and, in return for a monthly fee, secured us invitations to various VIP events in the capital. At first Tyson and I went along with it, persuaded it would benefit his career. We'd arrange for Mam to babysit Prince and Venezuela, and then drive down south to attend a product launch in Mayfair or a restaurant opening in Knightsbridge.

We quickly realised we didn't fit into this celebrity world. The VIP gatherings we went to felt so false; most guests were just there to pose for paparazzi, and their conversations with us went along the lines of 'Who are you? What do you do? Who do you know?' Tyson and I hardly had time to watch TV or read showbiz magazines (we still don't), so we had no real clue which boyband singer or reality show star we were chatting to or being photographed with. The other people at these events seemed to enjoy being part of the London social whirl – each to their own

– but, as far as we were concerned, it felt like a waste of our time and energy.

'This is pointless, Tyson,' I said after yet another disappointing evening. 'I could've had a great weekend at Mam and Dad's instead of hanging around with a bunch of strangers, just so we can get our faces in a magazine.'

'Agreed,' he said. 'It's a load of rubbish. Let's knock it on the head.'

We did, but not before one PR exec tried to persuade me to take part in a photoshoot for a tabloid newspaper. I remember thinking it was a bit odd, because Tyson was the famous half of the couple, not me. Call me naive, but not until someone mentioned 'swimsuit' did I realise that they were setting me up for some kind of Page 3-style shot. I refused point blank, of course.

'You're barking up the wrong tree,' I said. 'That's not my style.'

Tyson and I found the funny side of it, though. I wasn't going to get my kit off in a national newspaper just so he could raise his media profile and flog a few more fight tickets. From that time onwards, we purposely avoided the showbiz circuit, even when Tyson started to amass his titles and attract more attention.

Fast-forward to spring 2019, however – in the wake of Tyson's incredible boxing comeback – and a proposal arrived from a documentary-maker that attracted our attention. Tyson would regularly be sent programme pitches by television executives who thought his remarkable story would make him an ideal subject, and who'd ask him to consider taking part in a fly-on-the-wall TV show.

We always discussed these proposals together, because in principle we could see the potential benefits. Although we didn't really crave publicity, we realised that a documentary, if approached in the right manner, could actually do some good. On the one hand, it might give viewers the opportunity to see the 'real' Tyson Fury. Many people perceived him as a big, bad, loud-mouthed boxer (much of which was put on for show) but, as I knew more than anyone, in private he was a very kind, caring and compassionate man. On the other hand – and more importantly, perhaps – a documentary could also provide Tyson with the ideal platform to raise awareness of mental health issues, a subject that remained close to his heart.

Up until that point we'd turned down every approach. Some felt just too intrusive – we had our young family to consider, and a busy household to manage – and others seemed too time-consuming to fit in with Tyson's hectic schedule. A few producers were overly keen to focus on Tyson's Gypsy heritage, too, which rang a few alarm bells. While he was very proud of his Traveller upbringing – as was I – he had genuine and justified concerns about how he'd be portrayed.

Neither of us wanted our precious culture to be ridiculed for entertainment's sake, which I felt we'd already seen happen with programmes like *Big Fat Gypsy Weddings*, which I'd watched when the series first aired in 2011. It had caused a lot of upset and resentment among our community. Many of us felt it showed Gypsies and Travellers in a terrible light, focusing only upon a tiny section of people whose extreme and extravagant behaviour – from flashy weddings to rowdy gatherings – no doubt made for good television. However, the millions of viewers who tuned in and assumed all Gypsies followed similar lifestyles were being badly misled. The UK's Gypsy and Traveller population is extremely diverse, comprising dozens of distinct groups including English Romany Gypsies, Welsh Roma Gypsies, and Irish and Scottish Travellers like the Furys and the Mulroys. Each community has its own history, customs and identity, which they are rightly proud of.

I have to say, though, I hardly recognised any of the supposed Gypsy traditions featured in *Big Fat Gypsy Weddings*. For starters, in my community there was no rule that wedding dresses had to be the biggest and priciest creations you could get your hands on, unlike the huge, sparkly outfits paraded on the programme. Also featured on the show were instances of 'grabbing', a courtship ritual – usually at a social event – that involved a teenage boy seizing a girl he wanted to kiss. I'd never seen this myself, and I found it quite hard to watch. The whole intention was to poke fun at the Gypsy community, in my opinion, and there was no chance of me or Tyson participating in anything that peddled these misleading stereotypes. We both understood the fascination with Travellers – we're quite a private and secretive community – but we weren't going to set ourselves up to be mocked.

It was around the time of Adonis' birth that a production company called Optomen, who were working alongside ITV, approached Tyson with the proposal that finally interested him. They wanted to make an honest, in-depth documentary to show him in his true light, both as a dedicated athlete and as a devoted family man. It was pitched as a serious-minded programme, not a light-hearted reality show, that would steer clear of contrived storylines and staged scenarios.

'What d'you reckon, Paris?' said Tyson, as he handed me the proposal. 'This one looks pretty good.'

'Yeah, it does,' I said, flicking through the pages. 'Let's meet them.'

We clicked with Optomen's producer, Demi Doyle, straight away. Smart, genuine and enthusiastic, she listened carefully to our comments and concerns and reassured us of their intentions to create an authentic portrayal of his life and career.

'We're not trying to catch you out or show you up,' Demi told Tyson. 'We just want the world to see the real you, in and out of the boxing ring.'

Tyson decided to go for it. He signed on the dotted line and the documentary – *Tyson Fury: The Gypsy King* – became a reality. The camera crew would trail him over the space of a few months as he prepared for his fights, both in the UK and the US, and it was agreed he'd only be filmed at home when convenient.

The initial plan was to focus largely on Tyson's boxing career, and to minimise mine and the kids' participation. But once shooting began, this quickly became impractical. Every spare moment of Tyson's time at home was devoted to the family and, like many other households, we did all our activities together. So having replayed all the Morecambe footage in the editing room, Demi gave us a call.

'You guys are inseparable,' she said. 'It's virtually impossible to shoot Tyson at home without you and the children. And, if I'm honest, it wouldn't be a true reflection of his life if you weren't featured.'

Demi and the crew had noticed the strong connection between husband and wife, and they didn't want to gloss over it. They wanted me to have more input, they said, because the more they'd seen me and Tyson together, the more they'd realised there was a real love story going on. In their eyes, this documentary wasn't just about a boxer and his career; it was also about the woman who'd been by his side through thick and thin.

It was very kind of them to point this out, but I wasn't totally convinced.

'Are you *sure* you want me in this, Demi?' I asked. 'I thought it was just supposed to be about Tyson? Will the viewers really be bothered about me?'

'You'll have to trust me on this one,' she said with a smile. 'Just be yourself, and you'll be fine.'

After giving it some thought – and running it past Tyson – I agreed to allow the crew to film me as well. Demi had won my confidence, and I felt quite flattered to be included. I also gave them consent to include footage of the kids if they happened to come into shot – which was pretty often, as it happened – and I agreed to sit down for a couple of lengthy, face-to-face interviews that relived the highs and lows of our marriage. It was a very emotional experience. I really had to bite my lip as I opened up about my husband's mental health battle.

'He'd ballooned. He'd got to twenty-nine stone. He was drinking heavily. He was doing things I didn't even know about, and it was just getting out of hand,' I said, as the cameras rolled. 'It was a hard situation for anyone to be in.'

With the documentary now a family affair, I naturally became quite concerned about how we'd come across on screen. With five young children, two vocal parents and various friends and relatives coming and going, the Fury household could get very loud and chaotic. In the first week or so of filming I did my utmost to show us in a favourable light, continually cleaning the house, preparing nice, wholesome meals and reining in my unruly kids whenever their behaviour nosedived.

'Sit nicely, stay quiet, mind your language and do as you're told,' I'd warn them before I served up neat portions of cottage pie and vegetables. 'They're filming us, remember . . . I don't want people thinking we're a bunch of wild animals . . .'

This daft pretence didn't last long. After two or three days, I gave up. I was deluding myself. My ideal home and

picture-perfect family didn't exist, so I stopped the obsessive tidying, dished out nuggets and chips for tea and let the
kids run amok and be themselves. If this meant scenes of
chaos and clutter being broadcast to the British viewing
public, I'd just have to live with it.

One Saturday afternoon, when the film crew followed us
all into a local Italian restaurant, all five children had moods
and meltdowns. Venezuela was sulking, Prince and Baby
Tyson were having toy-related tantrums, Valencia was whin-
ing while trying to climb out of her high-chair and Adonis
was crying for his bottle.

'I'm really sorry about this,' I said to the cameraman as I
tried to wrestle my daughter back into her chair. 'They'll
calm down soon.'

'Don't apologise, Paris,' he replied. 'This is great. This is
real life.'

Most of the filming had finished by autumn 2019, when it
was time for Tyson to try his hand at a different sport. He'd
been a lifelong fan of WWE (World Wrestling Entertainment)
so when its head honchos, who in turn were big admirers of
his, invited him to join their star-studded USA show in the
gap before the Wilder rematch, he gladly accepted.

Not only was this a dream come true for Tyson, it was also
a massive deal for the children. My eldest boy was over the
moon when his dad told him the good news. Prince was a
huge WWE fan; he thought it was the best sport in town,
and had his own ambitions of becoming a wrestler.

'Wrestling's way cooler than boxing,' he'd often say to Tyson, before challenging his dad to a game of *WWE Superstars* on his PlayStation.

Part of Tyson's deal included his family being allowed to join him in America for the eight-week stint – he wouldn't have accepted it otherwise – and I wasn't exactly complaining. Before we left I also spoke with the children's school teachers, who kindly supplied me with some homework packs to keep them up to date with their class work.

The WWE organisation couldn't have been more welcoming. They flew all seven of us out to Los Angeles, first class – we usually travelled economy, so this was a proper treat – and we were put up in an amazing hotel in the city.

Tyson quite literally threw himself into the wrestling experience, making his first SmackDown appearance at LA's Staples Center (where he'd previously fought Deontay Wilder) by theatrically vaulting over a crowd barrier and grappling with WWE legends Dolph Ziggler and Braun Strowman. Although boxing and wrestling are very different disciplines – the first relies on punches to overpower an opponent, whereas the second uses locks and holds – Tyson took to WWE like a duck to water. The children and I had a brilliant time, holding aloft our giant foam 'thumbs-up' hands as we cheered on Daddy from our front row seats. I was so pleased the younger ones were finally able to see him in action, especially in a sport that was traditionally more theatrical and child-friendly than boxing. There would be no brutal and bloody scenes in these bouts.

Shortly afterwards we relocated to Orlando in Florida, where Tyson teamed up with the main WWE training camp. He had to prepare for his showpiece 'Crown Jewel' match against Strowman – scheduled for the end of October in Saudi Arabia – and in the meantime would continue making regular appearances on the WWE tour. The kids and I wouldn't be joining him in Saudi (they needed to return to school, and I had plenty of family-related matters to attend to) but this still left us with a fortnight of Florida sunshine to enjoy. While Tyson pumped iron in the gym, the rest of us chilled out at the hotel or the beach, and we'd all catch up later in the day to grab something nice to eat. When Tyson had a day off we'd visit Disney World, where they would lay on a fantastic VIP tour for us, usually reserved for the biggest names in showbiz.

There's no doubt about it, the Fury family were living the dream in Florida – so many fond memories were made that autumn – but, as parents, Tyson and I were conscious our children shouldn't take this amazing experience for granted. We were keen for them to appreciate how fortunate they were.

'Count your blessings, kids,' I remember telling them as we marvelled at the wonders of Disney World. 'Never forget how lucky you are.'

We met most of the big WWE superstars during our American adventure, including wrestling legends Ric Flair and Hulk Hogan. Even Tyson was a little star-struck when he came face to face with Dwayne 'The Rock' Johnson, although the feeling was clearly mutual. Dwayne turned out to be a huge fan of Tyson's; he knew all about his boxing career and really admired the way he'd staged his professional comeback. Tyson's story of recovery and revival tended to chime particularly loudly with other elite sportspeople; those who belonged to that world really appreciated the strength of character it took to turn around your fortunes.

Dwayne was a genuinely lovely man, and was so kind to the kids when we met him backstage after a show. He took time to talk to Prince about wrestling – my boy's smile had never been so wide – before happily posing for photographs with the whole Fury clan. Valencia was excited too, bouncing up and down in her pushchair when she recognised his voice from his role in *Moana*, an animated Disney film. 'Maui!!! Maui!!!' she shouted at him, which made us all laugh, Dwayne included – he slipped straight into character just for her benefit. It was a very sweet thing to do. Meeting mega-famous people can sometimes be disappointing – often they don't match your expectations – but The Rock certainly exceeded ours.

The WWE Crown Jewel, which saw Tyson facing Braun Strowman, the so-called 'Monster Among Men', took place in Riyadh on Halloween night. The kids and I watched it at my mam and dad's place, along with my brother Jimmy's children. All the youngsters were so excited to see their dad and uncle taking part in such a fantastic spectacle. Ever the showman, Tyson entered the arena dressed in an Arab robe

– the audience loved it – and, once inside the ring, he head-locked and power-slammed like he'd been wrestling all his life.

Watching him fight that night, while bouncing Adonis on my knee, I had a little moment of reflection. It was Halloween 2017 when I'd witnessed a sad, skeleton-suited Tyson return-ing home from a Morecambe pub, with the weight of the world on his shoulders. Two years down the line, here was my husband, a picture of health, strength and fitness, both in mind and in body. And, as he claimed an unlikely victory over Strowman with an impressive total knockout, our Tyson Fury Fan Club raised the roof.

A couple of months after his WWE success, Tyson resumed his boxing training in Las Vegas to prepare for the Deontay Wilder rematch. This time round, however, he'd be sparring without his coach Ben Davison. The previous fight against Wallin hadn't exactly gone to plan – questions had been asked about his fight preparation and his excessive weight loss, and he'd sustained that awful cut to his brow – and Tyson realised he'd need a change of direction if he was to stand any chance of beating Wilder. So he decided to join forces instead with Javan 'SugarHill' Steward, a more expe-rienced trainer who'd be able to work on his strength and technique and improve his punch-power. Ben was offered another role within the camp but for his own reasons decided not to accept, which Tyson fully respected. Happily, they parted on good terms and agreed to remain friends.

Ben had been instrumental in Tyson's mental and physical recovery – I don't think he'd have managed it without his help and support – and we both had lots to thank him for.

It was really tough being separated from Tyson but we spoke on the phone every day. He'd been joined in Las Vegas by his brothers Shane, Hughie and John Boy, as well as his cousin, boxing coach Andy Lee, who were all there to offer him extra support inside and outside the gym. His new regime was tough – it sounded like an army-style boot camp – but, by working with a different trainer and learning new things, he felt excited and revitalised, almost as if he was starting afresh. In fact, he was taking things so seriously he had some unexpected news for me.

'When you come over to Vegas I think you should stop in a hotel, Paris,' he said. 'Don't worry, I'll make sure you get the best room in town.'

The team wanted him to focus fully on the fight, he explained, and I felt my heart sink to my stomach. He didn't say as much, but I suspected they thought I'd be a distraction, in more ways than one. For us, though, staying together before a fight had become a ritual (a superstition, in fact) and I hated the idea of breaking it. But Tyson was clearly willing to do anything to win this fight, so I thought it best to hide my feelings and pretend I was OK with the decision.

'No problem, babe,' I fibbed. 'Whatever you think is best.'

Tyson kept his word as regards the hotel room. As soon as I landed at McCarran Airport, four days before the fight, I was whisked over to the MGM Grand in downtown Las

Vegas and was shown to a swanky suite in a private wing. Despite all the luxury, being apart from Tyson just made me feel anxious and irritable. I did my best to distract myself by going to a couple of the hotel's glitzy shows with friends and family (many of them had flown over for the fight, including my pal Cathy and my sister Montana) but I just wasn't in the mood for any after-hours partying. The others had turned their Vegas trip into a mini-holiday – who could blame them; they were in showbiz central – but I couldn't relax into it. The run-up to a fight was always a deadly serious time for me, and I never felt comfortable partying until it was all over. So, while the girls hit the Strip for a drink and a dance, I ended up watching TV in my suite or wandering around the hotel like a lost sheep. Occasionally I'd pass groups of raucous Fury fans sporting their Gypsy King T-shirts; thousands had landed in town for the big fight.

'Fury's on FIRE . . . Fury's on FIRE . . .' they'd chant, which was just making me miss him even more.

The only time we were able to spend together was an hour per day at Tyson's villa, after which I'd have to drag myself away. I'd become so used to being part of Team Fury, alongside his brothers and his coaching staff, and it felt weird not being involved this time round. My superstitious streak was getting the better of me, too. *Would this change be a bad omen? Would his good luck run out? Would his unbeaten record stay intact?*

On the eve of the fight it all got too much for me. I'd gone to see Tyson with Dave and Cathy – he was in great shape, and in good spirits – but as we drove back to our hotel, far from being relieved I was overwhelmed with worry. I felt just as jumpy for this Wilder fight as I had done for the first. Tyson may have exposed his opponent's weaknesses back in December 2018, but the Bronze Bomber remained a huge threat and still had the potential to cause my husband serious damage.

In the car, I could feel my stress levels rising. I suddenly burst into tears and punched the headrest in front of me so hard it skinned my knuckles; a classic Fury right hook. Our temporary separation may have helped Tyson's frame of mind, but it certainly hadn't helped mine. I didn't realise it then, but I think I was having a panic attack.

'I can't take all this,' I wailed, as tears streamed down my face. 'I hate not being with Tyson. I feel useless. It's *horrible . . .'*

Poor Dave had no idea how to handle me. It was so out of character. It took Cathy's intervention to finally calm me down.

'It'll be all right, Paris,' she said, gently putting her arm around my shoulder. 'I know it's been tough for you, but you've got to put your trust in Tyson. He knows what he's doing.'

The following day I still had a knot in my stomach, but thankfully I felt far less anxious. Tyson was keen to make the journey to the fight venue with me – I was glad at least to keep our tradition of arriving together – so I was given permission (thanks, team!) to get ready at his place. I changed into a full-length, off-the-shoulder red sequinned dress, which I complemented with a matching bag and a pair of red stilettos. Tyson's outfit was particularly snazzy; he looked amazing in a specially made Claudio Lugli white suit, covered with images of himself in various boxing poses.

The short trip to the MGM Grand, in a chauffeured Rolls-Royce, was totally bizarre – helicopters buzzed over us the whole way, as every metre of our journey was beamed live on TV – and it made me realise the true magnitude of the occasion. Wilder v Fury II had been billed as one of the most anticipated fights in a generation – a face-off between two undefeated champions, both in the prime of their lives, and at the peak of their careers – and would be watched by millions worldwide.

Both boxers had entered into a war of words in the build-up: 'You big dosser, you're getting knocked out,' Tyson had goaded in the pre-fight press conference, only for Wilder to respond with some pretty nasty references to mental illness. Tyson had then countered with a mocking rendition of Chumbawamba's 'Tubthumping' with its apt lyrics about getting knocked down and getting up again. Their fierce rivalry was genuine, not staged, and the boxing world could hardly wait to see them slug it out in the ring.

Despite all the fuss and fanfare, Tyson was as calm as ever when we finally arrived at the MGM. He was relishing the challenge and was ready for battle. I spent some time with him in the dressing room – I watched him getting his hands wrapped, and putting his gloves on – before giving him a good-luck kiss and going off to find my seat.

When he entered the Arena an hour or so later, Tyson was sitting on a throne dressed as a king and lip-synching to Patsy Cline's 'Crazy'. The sell-out crowd went wild with excitement – I'd never experienced an atmosphere like it – and the noise levels went through the roof when the bell rang to signal the start of the bout. I spent the first round to the last clinging onto the barrier in front of me, like I was on a white-knuckle rollercoaster ride. Squeezed in between Shane and Hughie, as per usual, I yelled my words of encouragement up to Tyson, flinching and gurning as each punch landed. I never look very pretty during a fight, it has to be said.

But that feeling that my husband could be knocked out at any second was truly frightening, as was the possibility that his brow scar could get reopened. Luckily it wasn't too long before Tyson's attack-minded training began to pay off. Towards the end of round three he knocked down Wilder, bombarding him with a flurry of punches that left him battered and bloodied. I never revel in any boxer getting hurt, but I did feel a tiny element of satisfaction in this case.

You had so much to say for yourself, Wilder, I thought to myself as he dragged himself up off the canvas. *You had this one coming . . .*

It was all over in the seventh round. Tyson's brute force and boxing brilliance left a dazed and disorientated Wilder on the ropes, and his corner wisely threw in the towel.

Following one of the greatest ever performances in modern times the WBC World Heavyweight title now belonged to my husband, and I couldn't climb into that boxing ring fast enough (not an easy task when you're wearing a skintight evening gown). Once the formalities were over Tyson treated the crowd to a rendition of 'American Pie', at one stage pulling me close to him and gazing into my eyes, as if to say 'I did this for us, Paris.' He knew I'd found things hard in Vegas but, in the world of top-flight sport, I also knew sacrifices sometimes had to be made. And as Tyson sang his heart out, with his title belt slung over his shoulder, that sacrifice suddenly seemed worthwhile. I couldn't have been more proud of my Gypsy King.

Our documentary – *Tyson Fury: The Gypsy King* – was eventually broadcast to the nation in the spring of 2020. Optomen had given us an advance viewing of all three episodes, with the option of making editorial changes if we wished, but as it turned out we didn't alter a thing. Some footage made me cringe – particularly a lovers' tiff Tyson and I had during a mini-break in Marbella, when I'd shed a few tears – but we had to agree it was an accurate reflection of Fury family life, warts and all. If we'd censored all the bits we weren't fond of, we wouldn't have been true to ourselves.

What really surprised me, though, was the amount of screen time that had been devoted to me. Even though I'd agreed to be filmed and interviewed, I genuinely hadn't expected to feature so heavily. And, as I watched the episodes unfold, I began to understand what Demi meant about our love story. We had never, ever styled ourselves as the perfect couple (at one point in the film I'd told him to f*** off during a phone conversation, when he'd stayed too long in the pub) but, despite the livelier moments, I think our deep affection for each other still really shone through. My husband said some very nice things about me – how I'd kept him going, and how I'd stood by him – and, in one really sweet scene, he dug out a pink polka-dot memory box I'd kept hidden in a cupboard for years. Among the mementos was a first-date cinema ticket for *King Kong*, a heart-shaped lollipop he'd bought me one Valentine's Day, and a yellow plastic 'engagement ring' he'd given me for a laugh when we were courting. He also produced a handwritten love note he'd once sent to me.

'In short, I will part with anything for you,' it read. 'There is only one happiness in life; to love, and to be loved.'

Prior to the documentary airing, I'd been asked if I'd help to promote it on national TV because, at that time, Tyson was in Vegas preparing for the Wilder rematch. I was more than happy to do so. I'd become quite accustomed to giving broadcast interviews, usually to the boxing channels that tracked Tyson's progress, and by now felt pretty comfortable in front of a camera. Tyson was fully supportive; he'd seen how confident I was in the spotlight, and knew I could rise to the challenge.

I was booked onto *This Morning* with Phillip Schofield and Holly Willoughby and *BBC Breakfast* with Charlie Stayt and Naga Munchetty and, the following week, *Good Morning Britain* with Richard Madeley and Ranvir Singh. The day before I was due on the *This Morning* sofa, I'd gone shopping in London for a new outfit with my friend Shannon. Mam had agreed to look after the kids for a couple of days, so I thought I may as well make the most of my trip.

'Oh, that's *such* a Holly outfit,' said Shannon as I tried on an unusual, ankle-length brown leather skirt in Zara. 'Smart and stylish, not too formal. That'd be perfect for the show.'

'Great,' I said. 'I'll take your word for it. I've got a cream shirt that'll go really nicely with it.'

The following day I arrived at the *This Morning* green room, only to see Holly Willoughby on the live TV feed wearing *exactly* the same brown leather skirt. I nearly fell off my chair.

She's got my skirt on! I said to myself. *She's going to think I've copied her!*

Her face was a picture when I walked on the set looking like some kind of Holly clone, but she took it all in good humour.

'Let's go shopping together, shall we,' she said, laughing, at the end of the interview. 'Nice twinning going on here . . .'

When *Tyson Fury: The Gypsy King* hit the screens, the public response was incredible. People seemed to enjoy this glimpse into our life – many commented that our family were more normal and grounded than they'd imagined – and the audience figures were excellent, apparently. But what heartened me most was the positive reaction to Tyson's frank account of his mental illness. He was overwhelmed by all the messages from fellow sufferers and their families who'd been touched by his story and identified with his experiences. He was also massively encouraged that it had even helped people seek professional help for their mental health problems, some for the very first time. Tyson had been so keen to use ITV's huge reach to promote the message that depression could affect anyone, even a world-famous boxer, and if this had prompted viewers to discuss their issues – especially men, who were often less likely to open up than women – then it really was a case of job well done.

In the weeks and months that followed, I lost count of the number of people who stopped Tyson in the street to wish him well, and to thank him for talking about a subject that had affected their friends or family. It brought it home to me how widespread this illness was, and how little it got discussed.

'You really struck a chord with my mum, she's been struggling with depression for years,' said one person as we walked through Morecambe town centre.

'My uncle went to see his GP after watching you, Tyson . . . I can't thank you enough,' said another.

There was a flip side to all this, though. In the final episode of the documentary, Tyson had posed for a selfie with a young twenty-something fan. After chatting to him for a few minutes, Tyson had rightly suspected the lad had suffered with mental health issues and had taken the time to offer him some advice, off his own bat (there were no parts of the documentary that were staged). It was a very powerful and memorable moment; the fan had promised to take his hero's words on board, and Tyson had been genuinely pleased to help.

However, once the programme had been broadcast, we began to receive notes through our letter box and knocks on our front door from people wishing to speak directly with Tyson, some of whom were in crisis. They'd seen his kindness towards that young man and assumed he'd be able to help them with their emotional problems, too. It put us in a really tricky position. While we had every sympathy with these individuals, we were simply unable to take on this kind of responsibility. In most cases we had to gently explain that, with the best will in the world, Tyson wasn't the answer to their problems, and we could only signpost them to their local GP. We also had our family and our privacy to consider. There were occasions when our eldest two had answered the door to strangers asking to speak to their dad, which was obviously a concern.

The notes and knocks tend not to happen nowadays and, while we're delighted Tyson has been able to raise awareness of mental illness, we continue to encourage anyone who needs help to seek support and guidance from a qualified health professional. It was only by doing so himself that Tyson was able to kick-start his own recovery.

Before the documentary was shown, I'd become used to being known as 'Tyson Fury's wife'. I'd always appreciated he was the famous half of the relationship – the superstar who everyone wanted to meet – and, when we were in public, I became accustomed to people blanking me and brushing past me as they made a beeline for Tyson. I never got upset or took it personally; fans can suddenly develop tunnel vision when they catch sight of a celebrity, and everybody else just fades into the background. I never saw myself as an accessory, or a trophy wife – and I always knew there was more to me than just dangling off my husband's arm, looking pretty – so I completely accepted the situation for what it was. I knew other wives of sports stars who didn't feel the same way, though; they felt constantly overshadowed, and hated being shoved out of the limelight.

'Ere, can you take a photo of us, luv?' was often the sum total of my interaction with Tyson's fans, who he'd often spend time chatting with because he appreciated their loyal support.

'Yeah, no problem at all,' I'd say, smiling, as they handed me their smartphone.

That all changed once *The Gypsy King* was televised. Almost overnight, and much to my surprise, people started to recognise me when I was out and about. In early spring 2020, a few days after the first episode had gone out, I was walking along Market Street in Manchester when I was tapped on the shoulder by a young woman in her twenties. Whenever I'm shopping in big cities with Tyson and the family we're likely to have security with us – it's a necessity these days – but on this occasion I was alone.

'Sorry to bother you, but you're Paris Fury, aren't you?' said the woman. 'I love your TV show so much. You and Tyson are *amazing*. Can I have a quick selfie?'

'With me? Are you sure?' I asked, genuinely taken aback.

The girl nodded, telling me she was going to post it on Instagram, and as I smiled into her phone camera I remember thinking how strange this all felt. In no way did I feel like a celebrity. I was just Paris: wife, mother, daughter, nurse, nanny . . .

Getting spotted in the street started to become commonplace and, in addition to the photo and autograph requests, something else began to happen. Men and women began to ask my advice, many of them husbands and wives of people suffering with depression. They'd seen me discussing Tyson's breakdown in the documentary, and being interviewed about it on *This Morning*, and wanted to know more about how, as his partner, I'd coped and kept myself on an even keel. I'm only too aware that we 'other halves' can feel very hurt, lonely and isolated, convincing ourselves we're the only people living this nightmare, and that no one in the world can begin to understand or empathise. I realised that by talking frankly about life with my troubled husband, I was reassuring others they weren't alone.

'So how did you get through it, Paris?' I'd be asked. 'What did you do to help yourself?'

While I'm more than willing to discuss my experiences with others, I'm also conscious that everyone's circumstances are unique. I'll never claim to be an expert on the subject of mental health, or to have all the answers and solutions; I'll leave that to the professionals. Neither would I dream of lecturing anybody about the right or wrong way to handle a scenario; I can only speak in terms of how I dealt with my own situation, and how I saw things from my perspective.

When Tyson was ill, I tried my best to stay strong. I am fully aware this can be easier said than done when you feel your world is crumbling, but I just knew I had to keep it together, for everyone's sake. With my husband struggling mentally and physically, and with my young children to look after, I had to hold firm, dig deep, and become the rock of the family. I'm not quite sure how I gained this inner strength and, to be honest, I think I surprised myself when I did. As a child I'd always been fairly shy and sensitive – my sister Montana was seen as the 'strong' one – but when the time came to tough it out as an adult I found I possessed more fight than I'd ever imagined.

Don't get me wrong, there were times when I felt myself wobble – usually when Tyson's behaviour tested me to the limit – but whenever this happened I'd just grit my teeth and push myself through the next hour, or day, or week. Over time, I learned to have trust and faith in my own strength. I realised I could cope with most things that were slung at me. As I'd often tell myself, 'God only gives us what we can handle.'

Throughout that difficult period, I knew it was vital for me to look after myself, in mind and body. Tyson had let himself go badly, and was leading a chaotic lifestyle, yet I was determined not to follow him down that path. I cared for myself as best I could; I ate well, I avoided alcohol and I tried to get a good sleep every night, although this was often scuppered by a restless child or an anxious husband.

Sticking to a rigid routine helped to keep me on the rails. Each morning I'd ensure I was up, washed and dressed before breakfast – even if I sometimes felt like slobbing out in my pyjamas all day – and would crack on with the normal daily agenda of school runs, food shops and housework. If I had time, regular walks in the open air, while pushing my babies along the beach in their double buggy, allowed me to clear my head and keep me fit. Maintaining this order and organisation in my life helped me to feel more calm and disciplined, even when other areas of family life felt totally out of my control.

Whenever I felt sad, scared or overwhelmed – quite normal reactions when your partner is unwell – I'd take myself to my 'happy place'. To me, this meant spending quality time with my children, indoors or outdoors. Whether it was playing ball games in the garden or cuddling up on the sofa to watch CBeebies, immersing myself in their world for a couple of hours gave me lots of comfort, and helped me switch off and wind down.

'Mammy, can we watch *Scooby-Doo* again?'

'We've watched that three times already today, Prince . . . how's about some Harry Potter instead?'

As time went on, I learned not to expect too much from myself, either, and tried to avoid piling unnecessary pressure on my shoulders. I came to see that Tyson's illness was a medical issue and, not being an expert in these matters, there was a limit to what I could do. I couldn't make him better or alter his behaviour – much as I'd have loved to – and I soon realised the best thing I could do was remain by his side and be there for him. Even in the worst of times, I knew we had a love worth fighting for, and I never gave up on him.

I also had to appreciate I'd sometimes get things wrong – I'm only human, after all – and, whenever that was the case, I didn't beat myself up about it. I had to learn not to be too tough on myself. I wasn't a doctor. I wasn't a counsellor. I was a young wife and mother who was just trying to keep her marriage, her family and herself together. In the early days of our relationship I remember using words like 'mad' and 'crazy' when Tyson was having an upper, or telling him to 'stop moping about' when he was on a downer. I still don't blame myself for that, though. I just said what I saw, using terms I was familiar with. I was only young, with no personal knowledge of mental health issues – I'd never heard of bipolar, or OCD – and I couldn't have been expected to understand Tyson's state of mind.

Looking back, if there's anything I'd have done differently it would have been to talk to friends and family. I really regret not doing this. For two long years I bottled things up and hid my feelings, embarrassed at the situation I'd found myself in and unwilling to burden my loved ones with my problems. In hindsight, opening up to Mam (or Montana, or

Cathy, or Shannon) would have given me a much-needed sounding board, and would have helped to lift the weight off my shoulders. I know they'd have listened to me, without passing any judgement, and would have offered me plenty of love and support.

So if you're reading this, and you ever find yourself in a situation similar to mine, I urge you to talk to someone. Please don't stay silent and cope alone; instead, pluck up the courage, choose the right moment and tell a friend or family member what you're going through. You could even speak with a health professional. By sharing your feelings with others, you'll be caring for yourself.

CHAPTER NINE

LIFE IN LOCKDOWN

PROMOTING *The Gypsy King* on TV had been great fun. Spending a few days in London had come as a refreshing change to my usual routine – I didn't get much 'me time' in my busy life – but not for one minute had I expected it to lead to anything else. In February 2020, however, just after I'd finished my interview on *Good Morning Britain*, I got chatting in the green room to a producer on *Loose Women*, ITV's long-running daytime discussion show. She told me she'd really enjoyed watching my chat with Richard and Ranvir – we'd covered all sorts of topics, ranging from boxing to parenting – and then asked me where I'd got my media training.

'Oh, I've never done anything like that,' I said. 'I've just become used to cameras and microphones being shoved in my face when I'm with Tyson.'

'Well, I have to say you're a natural,' she replied, 'and I'd love to have you on as a guest on *Loose Women*. Can I call you if we get a free slot?'

'Of course,' I said, slightly taken aback. 'If I can, I will.'

While I was really flattered by the invitation – I'd often watched the show myself, while giving the kids their lunch – I had to explain that I'd find it hard to commit to specific dates. Tyson's crazy schedule meant that life could be pretty unpredictable, and planning ahead was never easy. The producer totally understood, and we exchanged telephone numbers.

As things turned out, though, my chances of visiting the *Loose Women* studio any time soon went out of the window. By mid-March the coronavirus pandemic had finally hit the UK and the entire country had gone into lockdown. Like millions of other families, we all gathered in front of the TV and watched in shock as Prime Minister Boris Johnson told us we had to stay at home and follow the guidelines, which included limited social contact, severe travel restrictions and reduced outdoor exercise. It all seemed so scary and surreal – especially all the hand-washing and mask-wearing – and Morecambe, like most places, became a ghost town. And while I was really upset at the thought of not seeing my close friends and family, in particular my parents and siblings, my heart went out to the thousands of people who were in much worse positions, even losing their lives to this terrible disease.

Covid-19 caused the world of professional boxing to grind to a halt, too. The Fury v Wilder rematch had taken place a month before lockdown, but as the crisis deepened, and sporting arenas began to shut their doors to crowds, it seemed pretty obvious Tyson wouldn't be fighting for the foreseeable future. A third bout against Wilder, originally pencilled in for the summertime, was now highly unlikely to take place that year.

I was really worried about how Tyson would react to this setback. Without his usual targets to aim for and routines to stick to, I was concerned his mental health would plummet, just like after the Klitschko fight. Much to my relief, however, he managed this 'new normal' incredibly well. He accepted lockdown for what it was – an unprecedented situation that was totally out of his control – and prepared himself for a long break from competitive sport. Boxing, for once, would take a back seat. Like every parent in the country, Tyson's priorities – and mine – now lay in looking after our family and keeping them safe and well.

'This is bigger than me, this is bigger than boxing, this is bigger than sports,' he said in an interview at the time. 'So when the world gets back right again, then we'll talk about entertaining the customers and the fans.' I couldn't have agreed with him more.

But Tyson still had to find a way to keep fit. Exercise was his obsession – his well-being depended on it – and I think he was worried that, without that daily goal, his addictive personality would crave something else to fill the void, like overeating or binge-drinking. The thought of him relapsing terrified me, too.

'If I can't work out, I know I'll dip,' he told me. 'I've got to fill that gap somehow.'

The coronavirus situation had forced the closure of indoor leisure centres around the UK, and construction work on

Tyson's new, purpose-built boxing gym – based in the grounds of Morecambe Football Club – had come to a standstill. While he could still go for a run around the town, or along the shoreline, he was restricted to just one exercise period per day. So within days of lockdown being imposed, Tyson had borrowed a treadmill, which he installed in front of our living room window. I'd wanted him to put it in the garage, out of the way, but he told me he needed that lovely Morecambe Bay view to spur him on, and to make him feel he was running in the open air.

But his fitness masterplan wasn't going to stop there. Over breakfast one morning he told me he was going to devise his own exercise workout, which he was aiming to broadcast live from our front room to his Instagram followers. Mindful that many people were struggling to cope with lockdown, he wanted to find a fun way to help maintain everyone's mental and physical health. Crucially, it would also boost his own well-being and give him a reason to get out of bed every morning. It sounded like a brilliant idea, and I was very impressed.

'Good on you,' I said. 'Your fans will love it. So when are you doing it, then?'

'In ten minutes' time, at 9 a.m.,' he replied. 'And guess what . . . you're going to do it with me, too.'

'Not a chance, Tyson. I'm half asleep, I look a mess and I'm still in my pyjamas.'

'Oh come on, it'll be a laugh. We all need a bit of light relief at the moment.'

Tyson then led me into the front room, propped up his phone, pressed the record button, put on some background music and wished his Instagram Live followers a very good morning from Mr and Mrs Fury. And although I really wasn't in the mood, I joined in and followed his exercise routine as best I could, from stretches and lunges to sit-ups and press-ups. Tyson was a proper taskmaster – he was so strict, expecting me to match his own fitness levels – and I puffed and panted my way through the whole thing, flopping like a fish after each repetition. In my defence, being a busy mum meant I never had much time to do gym workouts. I generally kept in shape and burned off calories by running around after five children, which was no mean feat. On an average day I'd clock up twelve miles, according to the exercise tracker I wore on my wrist.

As the session progressed, the kids kept charging in and out of the lounge to see what all the fuss was about. Adding to the chaos was our yappy chihuahua, Minnie, who'd only joined our family a few months earlier.

God knows what all these viewers must think of all this mayhem, I said to myself as I noticed hundreds of Instagram 'Likes' appearing on the screen. *At least it's just a one-off . . .*

Or so I thought.

'So let's do this again tomorrow, people!' said Tyson, with a big grin, as he brought the routine to a close. 'We'll be here in the morning, same time, same place, won't we, Paris?'

'Yes, Tyson . . .'

I didn't have the heart to say no. My husband was clearly thrilled that so many people had tuned in, and I think he liked having me by his side for moral support. And if my presence was going to help him stick to a routine, stay in shape and stave off depression, then it could only be a good thing.

For the next three months, give or take the odd day off, I followed the same morning ritual. I'd get up early, sort out the kids' and the dog's breakfast, pull on a gym kit (yes, I ditched the pyjamas) and take part in the 'Gypsy Team' workout. As word spread, thousands of people began to log on from all around the world. Not only did they enjoy joining in with the star jumps and stomach crunches – everyone seemed to go fitness-crazy during lockdown – I think they also liked the chance to peer into the front room of a famous boxer and his wife.

Tyson and I certainly didn't put on any airs and graces – what you saw was what you got – and we bantered and bickered with each other while we exercised, like any married couple would. One morning we'd be totally loved up, linking arms and doing leg kicks, and the next morning we'd be scowling at each other, barely exchanging a word as we warmed up.

'This is what happens when you're in a marriage and you're locked in for three weeks together,' I said during one particularly stroppy session, when Tyson had wound me up by making me do ten sit-ups as punishment for turning up late.

The children continued to entertain our audience with their unscheduled on-camera appearances. Baby Tyson once wandered into the room with his trousers around his ankles and a roll of toilet paper in his hands, asking me to wipe his bottom, and his elder brother Prince had a massive melt-down one morning, calling his dad a very rude word beginning with 'p' before running away. Tyson may have laughed it off, but I didn't – I was fuming – and thousands of Instagram viewers saw me angrily dashing out of the door to give my eldest son a serious dressing-down.

Tyson had never intended to gain publicity from our daily workouts – they were just aimed at himself and his Instagram followers – but soon the media cottoned on to them, and he was asked onto *Good Morning Britain* (via Zoom, as had to be the case) with Piers Morgan and Susanna Reid. Towards the end of their chat he took the opportunity to give a heart-felt shout-out to the country's NHS workers, who were doing a fantastic job in terrible circumstances. Like much of the UK we had participated in the weekly 'clap for carers' on our doorstep, and Tyson had also joined forces with a health drink manufacturer to donate thousands of free bottles to hospital staff on the frontline. It was the very least he could do during these trying times.

As the weeks went by, I began to really see and feel the benefits of our Fury Family workouts. Tyson was full of praise for my efforts ('Paris, you are *super-fit*,' he said, as I lifted his dumb-bells with ease) and my strength and stamina increased tenfold. I reckon I was in my best shape for years – I found muscles I never knew existed – and each session got me fired up and energised for the rest of the day.

What also pleased me was the positive response I received from other women, including many fellow mums, who'd taken part in the workouts. A few of them said it was refreshing to see someone in the public eye who seemed comfortable with her 'normal' curvy figure – I've learned to love my chunky thighs – and others liked the fact I was happy to be filmed in all my unfiltered glory; most mornings I just scraped my hair into a loose ponytail and slicked on some lip balm. Even more encouragingly, some mums told me I'd inspired them to take up home exercise after they'd spent years shying away from gym classes for various reasons. If Paris Fury could prance around her lounge in her vest and leggings, getting all hot and sweaty, so could they.

One woman from the north-east even quit her daily drinking habit as a result of the workouts, and that prompted her into a total lifestyle change.

'I couldn't have done it without you two,' she said, when we congratulated her over a video call.

'It's so hard, but you've done fantastically,' replied Tyson, who knew only too well how difficult it was to break that cycle of dependency. 'Keep up the exercise. It's good for the mind, body and soul.'

The Fury Family Workout proved to be a resounding success, and Tyson was rightly proud of his efforts. Not only had his little brainchild improved people's well-being, it had helped to take their minds off the awful goings-on in the outside world (the World Boxing Council even gave us both a 'Heroes of Humanity' award for helping to raise spirits during lockdown). As things panned out, however, the sessions didn't continue into the second national lockdown, which hit the UK in autumn 2020. By that time sporting facilities had reopened for professional athletes, including Tyson's new gym in Morecambe, so he quite understandably returned to his regular fitness regime. I'd planned to carry on with the daily exercise routine in my own private time but, without my training partner by my side to urge me on, it just didn't materialise. As with most things in our life, Tyson and I worked so much better together.

The Fury family made the most of the first spring/summer lockdown. It was a rare opportunity for me, Tyson and the kids to spend precious time together, without any diversions or distractions. When you lead a busy life like ours, you find there's always someone or something pulling you in a different direction, and you hardly have a spare moment. Even when we holiday abroad there's always boxing-related business for Tyson to attend to, or paparazzi following us around, or tourists stopping to chat with their hero, so it can be hard to switch off and relax. Lockdown, of course, was an entirely different matter. For the first time in years, we found ourselves with a totally empty diary, free from fights, meetings and social events. It felt like a throwback to my childhood on Tilts Farm, where my family and I had led a very simple and slow-paced life, well away from the pressures and stresses of the outside world.

The gloriously sunny weather was a real blessing during lockdown, and we spent our daily quota of outdoor exercise exploring the local area. We'd always counted ourselves very lucky to live in such a beautiful part of the world – the Morecambe coastline is so unspoilt, as are the rolling Lancashire hills – but we'd never had the chance to discover it properly. So we took the opportunity to go on lots of long walks – usually down the canal or along the beach – and stumbled across many new sights and landmarks, including a big duck pond near our house that we'd never previously noticed. Tyson bought us all bicycles too, and one day I surprised myself by clocking up a seventeen-mile bike ride. I hadn't been on two wheels since I was a teenager, and I awoke the next morning feeling like my backside had been kicked by a Shire horse. After a while I got quite into it, though. One summer afternoon, when the UK lockdown had been briefly relaxed (and the kids were being looked after by Mam, who was in our 'support bubble'), Tyson and I cycled along the coastal path to the village of Heysham, where we stopped off to visit the ancient Viking tombs that are cut into the rock there.

'Isn't this lovely?' I said to him as we stood on the cliffs, admiring the views across the estuary. It felt really special to be in the middle of the countryside, just the two of us, with no one else in sight. We usually lived such a helter-skelter life, and this was a rare moment of peace and solitude.

With extra time on my hands during lockdown, and keen to ward off the 'Groundhog Day' boredom, I discovered a few other pastimes. I joined in the nationwide craze for cooking and baking, putting on my apron and making cupcakes and muffins with the kids and, much to Tyson's delight, presenting him with a raspberry pavlova that I'd been promising to make him ever since we'd got married, but had never got round to. I also perfected the traditional roast dinner. Prior to lockdown we'd eaten out every Sunday afternoon – it was my well-earned 'day off' from cooking duties – but, with our local pub closed due to restrictions, I soon got into the habit of ordering big joints of meat from the butcher and lovingly preparing lamb, pork or beef with all the trimmings. Cooking for just us seven felt very weird, though. Pre-Covid, our house had often been like Piccadilly Circus – there were so many comings and goings – and I'd regularly found myself setting extra places at the kitchen table for visiting friends, family or members of Tyson's boxing team. I looked forward to the day that I could see them all again.

For the first few weeks of lockdown, home-schooling took up a large-ish chunk of my time, too. At first we weren't sent too much study material by the kids' teachers – understandably so, since the lockdown had been so sudden – so I went into Morecambe to buy some maths and English textbooks for Venezuela, Prince and Tyson junior, as well as some colouring books for Valencia and Adonis. For the first fortnight or so I was like Supermam, overseeing my 'pupils' in the makeshift kitchen-based classroom while cracking on with the usual household chores.

'Right, you three, let's sit down and complete those exercises,' I'd say, getting out the pens and pencils and helping them as best I could. After a couple of weeks, however, it all went pear-shaped. The children got really bored with it all – all they did was sigh and yawn – and, despite my best efforts, I soon realised how rusty my maths and English skills were. One morning I decided to call it quits and apply my own brand of home-schooling.

'OK, kids. Who wants to learn about the insects and plants in the garden?'

'Me! Me! Me!' they all shouted, throwing down their pencils and rushing outside.

Even when the school began to send over proper, structured homework, I still carried on with the 'learning through play' activities. The kids and I made toys with tin cans and cereal boxes, staged our own Lego-building competitions and had loads of fun popping in and out of a 'jungle' tent in the front room. I put the tent up, of course, not Tyson. He's the world's worst when it comes to constructing things. We've had so many rows trying to assemble toy castles and garages in time for Christmas or the kids' birthdays.

'I know how to do this, I can see how this works,' he'll say, chucking away the instructions, before emptying all the screws and washers onto the carpet. Then, when he's halfway through – usually about three hours later – he'll lose his patience and fling everything at the wall, and that's when I'll take over and finish the job. I am one hundred per cent better at DIY than Tyson (I'll put up shelves and assemble flat-pack furniture, no problem) although he'll never admit the fact.

When the older children (briefly) returned to primary school in autumn 2020, I received a call from the *Loose Women* producer. She'd not forgotten our conversation earlier that year, and asked me if I was up for making that guest appearance we'd discussed previously, albeit remotely. I thought it'd be a fun thing to do – and Tyson was fine with it – so I was interviewed live from my kitchen in Morecambe, with a socially distanced ITV cameraman who'd made the trip up north. Ruth Langsford and the panel (Janet Street-Porter, Saira Khan and Coleen Nolan) asked me a variety of questions, including the story of how Tyson and I had first met, all those years ago.

'I was fifteen, he was seventeen, but he looked about thirty years old,' I said. 'People used to presume he was my dad . . .'

Towards the end of the interview, Tyson junior wandered into the kitchen and walked straight in front of the camera, much to my embarrassment and the panel's amusement. Some of the newspapers even ran it as a story the following day.

Despite my son's gatecrashing I must have made a good impression because, after the show, the producer asked me if I'd consider joining the *Loose Women* team as a regular panellist. They were happy to work around me – they appreciated I was a busy mam with limited childcare – and explained I'd be able to continue to participate via Zoom or

Skype, so wouldn't need to make the trip down to London (the lockdown travel restrictions would have made that pretty difficult in any case).

At first I didn't know what to think. This invitation had come totally out of the blue. Despite being married to one of the most famous sportsmen on the planet, I'd never actively sought to become a 'celebrity'. Being in the limelight had never topped my list of priorities. In the past, whenever an interesting opportunity had cropped up, I'd happily obliged – like publicising the *Gypsy King* documentary, or giving my post-fight views to a boxing channel – but I had no showbiz agent working on my behalf to find me jobs, auditions or endorsements. That still remains the case, as it happens; it's me who picks and chooses what I do, no one else.

I've actually turned down a few high-profile reality shows in the past, because they just didn't feel right at the time and, when it came down to it, I didn't want to spend long spells away from the kids. Tyson would have gladly taken over the childcare duties had I wanted him to – and he frequently encouraged me to take part in these programmes – but they just weren't for me.

Loose Women was another matter, though – it was definitely something I could work around – and the more I mulled things over, the more I realised it could be a positive step forward.

You've got a voice, Paris . . . why not use it? I said to myself.

I could speak up for the millions of multi-tasking mums out there – I knew how tough parenting could be – and also for the many wives and girlfriends who'd supported their partners through depression. And, as one of the few Traveller women in the public eye, I could also use this national platform to proudly fly the flag for my community. Not that I'd ever claim to be a mouthpiece for every woman with Gypsy heritage, of course – ours is a very diverse group, full of different opinions and experiences – but I liked the idea of my mere presence on the panel breaking down a barrier or two.

So, having weighed it all up, I decided to go for it. Tyson was so proud when I told him.

'That's brilliant, Paris,' he said. 'My wife . . . a Loose Woman!'

'I know . . . who'd have thought it?' I smiled.

I made my debut as a panellist in November 2020, along with Jane Moore, Stacey Solomon and Linda Robson. The team couldn't have made me feel more welcome – it felt like a real sisterhood – and, despite a surge of nerves when the opening credits rolled, I soon got into my stride. Sitting in my front room, with Morecambe Bay as a backdrop, I joined in the conversation and offered my views on topics ranging from mums doing school runs in pyjamas to men looking after their mental health. Tyson had of course given me his blessing to discuss his own experiences with the latter; as far as he was concerned, the more this subject was talked about, the better.

'I think Tyson opening up about his issues has helped people to come forward and say "well if he can say it, I can say it,"' I explained. 'Bottling it up is not a good thing. Always try your best to let your feelings out. Never feel ashamed or embarrassed about what you're thinking or feeling.'

In many ways, I think my Traveller background and beliefs worked to my advantage on *Loose Women*, since I was able to approach certain matters from a different angle. I'm well aware that my outlook on life can be quite traditional – some might even say old-fashioned – and this often put me at odds with the other panellists. But it generally made for 'good television', as they say.

A case in point was the issue of secondary education, which Tyson and I had memorably argued about in the *Gypsy King* documentary while discussing the children's future schooling. In the past it's been a real bone of contention between us, since we have such opposing views. Tyson's attitude has always been more open and relaxed than mine. He's never objected to the idea of our children attending high school at the age of eleven and thinks far too many Travellers are held back by a lack of education, while other minority groups embrace it to their advantage. He's keen for our kids to widen their opportunities as much as possible so they can reach their full potential in life.

I'm not convinced that secondary school is the answer to everything, however, and I firmly believe you can be successful with or without it. If push came to shove I'd much rather my children followed the traditional Traveller route by spending those five years at home instead, just like I did. I still cherish my Gypsy values, and I feel it's my duty to educate my kids about our ways and customs, so they're not forgotten and can be passed down the generations. I'd also argue that leaving school at eleven never did Tyson and me any harm; I think we're both pretty switched-on people who've done all right for ourselves.

Thankfully, Tyson and I have recently buried our differences and reached a compromise. We've agreed that our children will be home-tutored by specialist teachers when they leave primary school, which means they can study towards academic qualifications like other pupils, just not within a school environment. And when they turn sixteen, they can decide for themselves whether they continue their education or choose a career. It's an outcome that Tyson and I are equally happy with. The best of both worlds.

The *Loose Women* team had seen us locking horns in the documentary, though – at one point Tyson had referred to me as a 'dream killer', which was a bit harsh of him – and panellist Janet Street-Porter was particularly keen to quiz me further on the subject.

'So what if Venezuela wanted to be a brain surgeon, something that you couldn't teach her at home?' she asked, a little mischievously.

'I wouldn't take that opportunity away from her. The possibility for her to carry on studying will always be there,' I said, explaining that, even if my daughter left school at the age of eleven, she could still attend further education college in the future, as I'd done myself.

Although Janet and I agreed to disagree on many *Loose Women* talking points – her views are a bit more liberal than mine, shall we say – I really liked and respected her. Some of my friends who'd watched the show got the wrong impression, however, and assumed there was bad feeling between us.

'Why is Janet always on your case, Paris?' they asked. 'She's forever having a go.'

'Don't be daft,' I replied. 'It's just healthy debate. We're both straight talkers. I think she's great.'

Maybe I was a little *too* plain-speaking sometimes, though. During one show, I mistakenly blurted out that 'the shit hit the fan' as Jane Moore quizzed me about the comings and goings of our chaotic family life. I didn't know what I was thinking – I couldn't believe I'd sworn on live TV – and I felt myself blushing from top to toe. I offered the team a heart-felt apology when we eventually came off air.

'Hey, these things happen, Paris,' said Jane, smiling. 'Don't worry, we've all done it.'

'That makes me feel a bit better,' I said, grateful to be working alongside such kind and forgiving women.

But that was an isolated slip-up. Other than that, I think I did OK. I didn't go onto *Loose Women* expecting to be everyone's cup of tea – I don't exactly sit on the fence – but, nevertheless, it was really nice to receive some positive feed-back on social media.

'You're a breath of fresh air, Paris,' posted one viewer. 'I love how you say what you think, it's so rare these days.'

'For someone who gave up formal education at eleven she sounds very wise and articulate,' said another. Many Traveller women got in touch, too, saying it made a nice change to turn on the telly and see someone who they could not only identify with, but who was also sticking up for their community.

But it wasn't all balloons and bouquets and, inevitably, a few haters crawled out of the woodwork. It wasn't very nice reading social media posts like 'Who's this pikey on the panel?' and 'Where will she park her caravan?' but I dealt with these trolls in my usual way – by ignoring them and refusing to bite. If an anonymous stranger from cyberspace tells me that dirty gyppos shouldn't be on television, it's in one ear, out the other. Sadly, anti-Traveller comments like these are still pretty commonplace. Intolerance and discrimination has always been a part of my life and, unfortunately, probably always will be.

I won't delve deep into the history of Gypsy and Traveller prejudice – it's a story of hardship and hostility that goes back hundreds of years – but, as someone who had a conventional Gypsy upbringing, maybe I can try to explain the difficulties we face. Coming from a traditional Traveller family, I always grew up feeling that the outside world, the non-Gypsy 'Gorger' people, didn't seem to accept or understand our ways and customs. We might have looked like them, and spoken like them, but our lifestyles differed so much – from living in trailers to leaving school early – and I always had the sense that we were poles apart.

Over time, mistrust and suspicion has built up on both sides, which has often culminated in tension between us. Some non-Gypsies see us as aloof and secretive – I'd prefer to say private and self-sufficient – because we close ourselves off from wider society and abide by our own set of rules and customs. By the same token, many Travellers are brought up to feel wary of the outside world, perhaps due to the way our people have been mistreated through the generations. We assume (perhaps wrongly sometimes) that we're hated from every direction, and we put up barriers to protect ourselves and, in doing so, are probably less likely to integrate than other minority groups. Ever since I can remember, there's always been a 'them and us' sense of detachment between Gypsies and non-Gypsies.

'Okay, we get it . . . you clearly don't like us, so we'll just live our own lives, stick with our own people and keep out of your way,' is a Traveller mindset I'm very familiar with.

Sometimes, to avoid any hassle and harassment, we've taken special measures to protect ourselves. I vividly remember my parents telling me not to tick the 'Gypsy/Traveller' box when I filled out a form, whether it was for a bus pass or a cinema membership. This wasn't because my family didn't want me to be proud of my culture and identity – they truly did – but it was more to prevent me from suffering the discrimination this label might bring.

'If you want an easier life, Paris, put your X in the "White British" box,' I'd be told. So I always did.

When we started going out socially, my teenage friends and I became used to being turned away from cinemas, skating rinks and bowling alleys, simply because of our background. One large entertainment complex appeared to operate a 'No Travellers' policy, which they'd tighten up at weekends. Since Doncaster was a town with a historically large Traveller population, you might have expected local venues to be more tolerant and welcoming but, back then, groups of Gypsy girls seeking a fun day out were often made to feel like trouble-causing lowlifes.

'Why can't we come in? We just want to go bowling.'

'Sorry. I'm not allowed to let in any Travellers today.'

'How d'you know we're Travellers?'

'I just do. Now could you leave the premises, please?'

As someone born and bred into that community, I can spot a fellow Gypsy from a mile off, whether I'm at home or abroad, and I can only presume these bouncers had a similar ability. I can't put my finger on it – it's not as if we have distinctive skin tones or facial features – you just *know*. It's a vibe, a feeling. Often the other person will have the same sense of recognition, and you'll exchange a quick smile and a nod of understanding.

I know you're a Gypsy, you know I'm a Gypsy . . . how's it going?

My girlfriends and I soon wised up to the fact that it was much easier to get into these venues if we separated out and queued up in pairs. A large group of us would often act as a red flag to the bouncers, so we'd gather quietly in twos and threes before gaining entry and reuniting in the skating rink or the bowling alley. I very much doubt that groups of non-Gypsy girls were forced to go through a similar *Mission Impossible*-style rigmarole every Saturday.

The anti-Gypsy prejudice continued when I got together with Tyson. I lost count of the times when, in our late teens and early twenties, we'd arrive at restaurants in Doncaster or Lancaster, only to be told they were only accepting bookings that night, or hadn't got any tables available. But you'd know full well they were fibbing. As you walked away you'd see the couple behind you being waved in without a reservation, before being directed to one of the many empty tables inside the restaurant.

'Bare-faced liars,' I'd say to Tyson. 'Could they have made it any more obvious?'

'Ignore them,' he'd reply. 'They're just small-minded people. Don't worry, we'll take our business elsewhere.'

Things changed once Tyson started to win titles, and his fame began to grow. Not long after our marriage, we paid a visit to a nightclub in the north-west of England and – shock, horror – we were refused entry at the door, for no valid reason. However, when the owner found out afterwards that a champion boxer had been barred from his venue, he got straight in touch with Tyson to offer his apologies. He admitted the local police had warned his staff to send Gypsies packing, and they were just following orders.

'I'm so sorry, mate,' he said. 'If I'd known it was you at the door I'd have made an exception. You must visit us again, and this time I'll make sure you're looked after.'

'Well, that's really good of you,' said Tyson, sarcastically. 'So you're happy to let me in because it looks well on your club, but you wouldn't do the same with my friends and family? Thanks, but no thanks.'

A decade down the line, I'd like to say that things have improved in this area, but I'm not convinced. Although the days of Tyson and me being turned away from restaurants are long gone – he's so well-known now, the exact opposite is the case – I still hear disturbing stories about venues refusing entry to other members of the Traveller community. In one town, I'm told, local officials advised every single pub landlord to close their doors on the day of an Irish Traveller funeral, assuming there'd be trouble, and implying the police wouldn't intervene if this was indeed the case. The landlords did as they were told, and the funeral-goers were unable to give their beloved friend a proper send-off.

And, nearer to home, Tyson lent his support to a group of locals who claimed they'd been barred from a pub due to its No Travellers policy, although once the story hit the media the brewery begged to differ. I'm not suggesting every Gypsy and Traveller is an angel – we have our bad apples, like most sections of society – but, all too often, decent and right-minded members of our community are tarred with the same brush.

Traveller prejudice isn't just confined to the hospitality industry in Britain, though. A well-known holiday park was recently exposed for compiling a blacklist of common Irish Traveller surnames so they could screen out bookings, and I know of many Gypsy people who are still being turned away from a string of shops and salons, for no reason other than their heritage.

Sometimes casual racism can happen when you least expect it, as I experienced myself a couple of years ago. One afternoon, my friend Cathy and I went for a drive around Morecambe to look at a few houses for sale (now that the family had started to outgrow our place I was starting to keep tabs on the property market). As we drew up outside a spacious detached house, and got out of the car to take a closer look, a woman in her seventies shuffled out. She proceeded to give us a potted history of the property; when it was built, what work had been done on it, that kind of thing.

'. . . and believe it or not, the previous owners were Gypsies,' she said.

'Oh, really?' I replied, giving Cathy a dig in the ribs and a 'bet-she-doesn't-know-we're-Travellers' look.

'Yes, they were. But luckily they weren't those scummy gyppos,' she said. 'They were those posh gyppos.'

'Ah, the *posh* gyppos. What a relief, eh?' I said, winking at my friend. 'Anyway, thanks for the chat . . . we'd better be on our way.'

Me and Cathy burst out laughing as we walked back to the car, probably more out of shock than anything. We couldn't quite believe what we'd just heard. However, as I reflected on it later, I felt cross that I hadn't spoken up for myself. This woman's words were really offensive and shouldn't have been tolerated. Someone from another culture in a similar situation might have taken her to task, and rightly so. However, in my experience, all too often we Gypsies turn a blind eye to bigotry. We almost expect to be treated like dirt – we normalise it, in a way – and we are far more likely to shrug our shoulders than stamp our feet. There is almost a weariness on our part, a resignation that society views Travellers as the lowest of the low, and we should just suck it up and move on. But we shouldn't. It's unacceptable. It's as bad as any other prejudice.

These days, Tyson and I are trying our best to change this mindset, in public and private. My husband's amazing success in the boxing ring has proved that people from our community can overcome barriers and achieve great things, while still staying true to their roots. By celebrating his herit-age on an international stage – and by revelling in his 'Gypsy King' persona – he has encouraged Travellers around the world to stand tall and take pride in their birthright.

And, as far as I'm concerned, I'm happy to use whatever platform I've got – the occasional TV appearance, and the book you're reading right now – to give an insight into my background, and to explain how it's shaped my outlook and influenced me as a person. My lifestyle and circumstances may have been transformed since those Tilts Farm days, but I still hold my Traveller values dear and feel privileged to be a member of that community.

As parents, protecting and preserving our Gypsy culture is an important part of our lives, too, and Tyson and I will continue to teach our children to respect our traditions, honour our customs and embrace our values. We hope they'll grow up with such a strong sense of identity and belonging that, one day, they'll be able to tick that 'Gypsy/ Traveller' box with pride.

The second coronavirus lockdown, which came along in the autumn and winter of 2020–2021, proved to be much harder to bear than the first. The cold, wet weather put paid to most of our outdoor activities (that coastal wind could be biting) and the Fury family spent much more time cooped up indoors. The primary schools had closed their doors again – like many parents, I really missed that six hours of breathing space – and, with the kids running around the house like caged animals, I started to feel the strain.

'To every mother and father who are in lockdown with a few kids at home, I salute you,' I said on an Instagram Story, which I'd filmed while making tea with noisy kids in the background. 'I'm feeling it too . . . it's hard work.'

I was hugely concerned about Mam and Dad, too, who'd both contracted coronavirus; they were quite poorly at first but made a full recovery, thank goodness.

The new lockdown derailed Tyson, too. Earlier that year, during the summer lifting of restrictions, a fight had been arranged for Saturday 5 December at the Royal Albert Hall in London. He was due to face German Agit Kabayel – there was no title to fight for, but it would be a good test against a highly rated boxer – but, due to the pandemic, the action would take place behind closed doors and without crowds. Tyson was beyond excited; it was going to be his first fight in more than a year. He swiftly set up a training camp at his new gym in Morecambe, which had finally been completed in the summer, and – because it fell within the category of work – he was able to fly his coach SugarHill Steward over from Detroit, as well as a nutritionist and a couple of sparring partners.

All the hotels were closed, however, so the only option was for the entourage to move into our house with Tyson for a couple of months, while me and the kids moved out. I didn't mind at all. I was used to upping sticks at a moment's notice and actually felt relieved that Tyson finally had a fight to focus on. So I loaded all our belongings into the van and drove the children over to our holiday home in the Midlands, which we'd bought to use as a base when I visited my parents (it was situated right next door to their place). I'd yet to furnish the property – the sale had only recently gone through – so I had to hastily kit it out with TVs, beds and sofas.

Mam, Dad and Romain had moved out of their Doncaster house a few years earlier and relocated to this gated Traveller site – I think they'd missed being in the thick of the community – and were now living much closer to my brother Jimmy, my sister Montana and their families. My kids came to love their visits to Granny's place, and it was great to see them having outdoors fun with their friends and cousins, and living an authentic Traveller life. My Midlands base was a proper home-from-home, perfect for getting away from it all and catching up with my family.

I was back in Morecambe sooner than expected, though. Tyson's fight in London was suddenly cancelled, only a month before it was due to take place. Various problems had prevented it from going ahead, apparently; many hurdles have to be overcome when setting up a boxing match, and sometimes things just don't work out. So SugarHill and the entourage returned to America – living in Morecambe had been a whole new experience for them – and back home I came with the kids. It was a major blow for Tyson, who just couldn't believe all that time and effort had come to nothing. It really knocked him for six.

I could tell within minutes of walking through the door that he was in a bad place. Since his breakdown a few years earlier I'd taught myself to recognise the signs – I could see it in his eyes, and hear it in his voice – and I felt more able to confidently handle the situation. I'd also learned not to tell him to snap out of it, or pull himself together, as I'd done in the early days of our marriage, when I'd had no understanding of depression. I knew the best course of action was to stay by his side, offer my support, and let him know he was loved.

That evening, once the kids had gone to bed, I sat down with him and talked things over.

'I can feel myself falling again,' he said. 'I don't want to go to that dark place.'

'I'm here for you,' I replied, giving him a big hug. 'We'll get through this.'

After a fortnight or so his mood seemed to lighten a little, even though he still felt unable to train every day. But as Christmas approached – usually his favourite time of year – I could see he still wasn't firing on all cylinders. Morecambe could be a bit grey and dismal in December, so I wondered whether we should get away for a few weeks. I knew Tyson had some business to do in America, so I suggested we all spend the festive period in Miami, a city we all adored, while he had his meetings. The warm sunshine would do him good, I reckoned, as would a change of scenery. In normal circumstances I'd have much preferred to stay at home and celebrate – we'd had enough moving around in the last few weeks – but Tyson's health was my top priority. He was thrilled with my plan – his eyes lit up when I mentioned it – and within hours he'd booked our hotel and flights, while checking we met all the visa and Covid-19 regulations.

Unfortunately, I didn't enjoy the trip at all. While the winter sun in Florida was lovely, and proved to be a welcome tonic for a much happier Tyson, I found our stay far from relaxing. Whenever we went down to the hotel's pool area we'd be besieged by other holidaymakers, all wanting to chat and take photographs. We had no privacy whatsoever – it felt like we were constantly on show, like animals at a zoo – and after a while it became unbearable. In hindsight it was our own fault; we should have known this was going to happen, and should have booked ourselves into a secluded villa rather than a crowded hotel. Daft as this may sound, sometimes we forgot just how famous Tyson was, and how much of a commotion he'd cause. It was a lesson learned.

Christmas Day proved to be the final straw for me. It couldn't have been less traditional. The previous day we'd asked our hotel concierge to book us in for a proper, British-style Christmas dinner in the restaurant, only to be told that it was served from 5 p.m. onwards, which was a lot later than we'd hoped.

'Can we reserve a table for Christmas lunch instead?' we asked.

'Lunch tomorrow, of course,' he said. 'I'll book you in for noon.'

We spent the morning getting dressed up in our best outfits and rocked up to our table in what turned out to be an almost empty restaurant. We were then handed the menu: sushi, hamburgers and chicken tenders, everything you'd expect to see on a Florida menu. No turkey, stuffing or cranberry sauce in sight. The traditional Christmas dinner was only being served in the evening, the waiter informed us – which was now fully booked – and their lunchtime options remained the same as usual.

'Sushi for me and my wife, please,' said Tyson, who took it all in good humour. The kids weren't bothered, either; they were more than happy with burgers, fries and ketchup.

I didn't enjoy it at all, though, and as I imagined my family in the UK sitting around a festive table, tucking into turkey and pulling Christmas crackers, I felt a sudden wave of homesickness.

'I don't want to be here,' I whispered to Tyson, as tears sprang to my eyes. 'I want to go home.'

I couldn't understand why I felt so upset. There I was, spending precious time with my beloved family in the Sunshine State, but still getting all weepy about a Christmas meal. Nothing was that important, surely; it felt like proper spoilt-little-rich-girl stuff. But a few days later, when I discovered I was pregnant with our sixth child, my wobbly emotions all made perfect sense.

Just after New Year's Day we found ourselves heading back home to the UK, a week earlier than planned. The relief was immense on my part. I couldn't have been happier to swap Miami for Morecambe.

CHAPTER TEN

LOOKING GOOD

Finding out I was pregnant with baby number six wasn't a huge surprise, if I'm honest. Towards the end of 2020 Tyson and I had discussed trying for another child, especially now Adonis was almost two and nearly ready for nursery, although we'd not expected to conceive so quickly. We were both thrilled to bits – becoming parents was still the best thing in the world – but not everyone in the family shared our enthusiasm. Our eldest, Venezuela, was seriously unimpressed when we told her she was going to have another baby brother or sister, screwing up her face as if to say 'Really? Does this crazy family need any more kids?' After a bit of cajoling, though, she eventually came round to it.

I had hoped to announce my baby news publicly on *Loose Women* in February, about three months into my pregnancy, but – as per usual – Tyson opened his big mouth beforehand and stole my thunder. He'd been unable to contain himself; he was just so giddy with excitement he blurted it out during an interview with a boxing journalist he knew well.

'Paris is pregnant again . . . the Lord has blessed us with another child,' he said, and as soon as the interview was released my phone began to buzz with messages.

It was still nice to share my glad tidings on *Loose Women*, even though the cat was now well and truly out of the bag. My fellow panellists were all really pleased for me and showered me with good wishes.

'What lovely news, Paris,' said Jane Moore. 'Such a nice tonic in these grim times.'

When Tyson and I attended the sixteen-week gender scan at a private clinic, we'd already decided we didn't want to be told the sex of the baby face to face. The clinic had started to offer a novelty 'gender reveal' option whereby the sonographer would identify whether it was a boy or girl – but not tell the parents, instead handing them a special confetti cannon (with either blue or pink contents) that they could take home to reveal the news to family members. Tyson and I had never done this before, but there was a first time for everything, and we thought it would be nice to involve the children. So while the scan took place we both turned away from the screen and closed our eyes, before taking receipt of our very own confetti 'popper'. We had no idea if it was pink or blue.

'I'll be just as happy with a boy or a girl, you know,' I said to Tyson as we drove back home. He agreed; as had always been the case, our main concern was for our baby to be healthy, whatever its gender.

Once Tyson had picked up the older kids from school, I got ready for the big reveal. I couldn't wait to surprise everyone, and set up my phone's camera to capture this hugely emotional family moment. With all seven of us gathered in the hallway, I began the countdown.

'Three . . . two . . . one . . .' I shouted, and pulled the trigger, which released a huge shower of pink confetti. '*It's a GIRL!* We're having another little princess!'

Let's just say it didn't have the desired effect. In fact, the whole thing was a total and utter flop. Four out of the five kids' faces were like wet weekends – Prince was the only one who wanted a little sister – and, while Tyson was delighted, I got the feeling he thought this confetti cannon was all a bit OTT. To cap it all, I hadn't realised this popper blasted out puffs of fluorescent pink powder – it went absolutely everywhere – and I spent hours trying to clean it off the floor tiles afterwards.

'What a waste of time. I don't know why I bothered,' I muttered as I scrubbed the stains away. 'I won't be doing this again.'

'You might have to, if we have another five kids,' said Tyson. He'd always said he wanted us to produce enough children for a family football team.

I still posted a photograph of our big gender reveal on Instagram, though, despite it not exactly going to plan, and was blown away by the thousands of kind-hearted messages it received. After such a miserable year, I think people were keen for any good news they could find. Many well-wishers really liked the fact we were evening up the male/female balance in the family; three boys and three girls seemed perfect to me, too.

I'd first dipped my toe into the world of Instagram back in August 2012. Of all the social media platforms available, it quickly became my favourite. I'd found it a bit kinder and gentler than Twitter (there were too many trolls on there for my liking) and, compared with Facebook – which I mainly used to stay in touch with friends and family – it was faster and easier to connect with lots of people and share my news and photos. I'd set up my account just for a bit of fun, really, using it to upload snapshots of my favourite people, places and possessions; one day it could be a cream cake I'd brought home from my local Greggs, the next it could be a pair of shoes that I'd bought from Harvey Nicks. Children's birthday parties, meals out with Tyson and shopping trips with my friends all got the Instagram treatment. I soon built up a large following – maybe a hundred thousand or so within a few months – although in the early days I did wonder how many of them were just boxing fans, hoping to catch a glimpse of their sporting hero.

Once I'd got the hang of it, I started to post some hair and make-up tips on my timeline. I'd seen other users do the same, and thought I may as well give it a go. Although I'd called time on my beauty therapy work in my teens – I'd happily chosen to become a housewife instead, and focus on Tyson's career – my interest in that field had never faded and I still loved experimenting with new looks, styles and products. As a busy mother I rarely got the opportunity to visit high street salons – it could be every six weeks, when I got my hair done – so I found myself doing lots of DIY pampering instead. I started to upload photos of the end result – often when I was on a date night with Tyson, when I'd be looking all glossy and glamorous – and I'd be deluged with messages from followers asking for my beauty hints. As I didn't have time to respond to them all individually, I began instead to post short, chatty, step-by-step videos – Instagram 'stories' – in which I shared my suggestions and recommendations, often giving shout-outs to my favourite products and appliances.

'Hi, it's Paris Fury here, I just thought I'd show you my signature hairstyle,' I'd say to my followers, propping up my phone before demonstrating how straightening irons could be used to create long, bouncy curls. It's a really useful tip that I love to pass on to others; there's a proper knack to it, which comes from lots of practice. My various beauty hacks were going down well, and I received really positive feedback from women all over the world. It felt great to be doing something off my own bat for a change – I was proving again I was more than just 'Tyson's wife' – and I liked the idea that my advice was helping time-starved mums to look and feel better.

When *The Gypsy King* was first broadcast in February 2020, and my face became more familiar on television, my Instagram follower count shot up to half a million. I even saw myself being referred to as an 'influencer', but as far as I was concerned I was just a wife and mam having a bit of fun in my spare time.

I love being part of the Instagram community, though; it's a really friendly social network and there are some fantastically talented and creative people on there. And as long as I keep on enjoying it – and my followers still like what I'm doing – I'm more than happy to carry on posting.

When people ask me about my beauty routine, they're often pretty surprised when I tell them how simple and straight-forward it is. For me, everything has to fit into a busy life-style – I haven't got time for much faffing about – and I certainly don't believe in spending money on expensive products when it's really not necessary. You don't have to break the bank to look your best.

The women in my family have always taken a great deal of pride in their appearance. When I was younger my mam didn't have a very posh or fancy lifestyle, but she always looked immaculate, and still does. She bought quality, well-made clothing that lasted well, and sometimes even ran up her own outfits using her beloved sewing machine. Whatever she had planned for her day, even if she was just smartening up the trailer, she'd style her hair, put her 'face' on and dab on some perfume. This made a real impression on me – I loved watching Mam go through her little routine every morning – and I've since followed in her footsteps. I can be popping to Asda, or doing the school run, but beforehand I'll always apply some blusher and lip gloss, give my hair a good brush and spritz on my favourite scent. It only takes seconds but it makes me feel nice, fresh and ready to face the day. And while I won't get dressed to the nines for every-day comings and goings – it's all about comfort and practicality when you're a busy parent – I'll still wear a nice pair of jeans, a smart top and a clean pair of trainers.

Even when I'm indoors, I try not to spend too much time in leggings and joggers, unless I'm doing jobs and chores (or I'm on a fitness kick). Mam always brought me up to look smart and presentable and, as I grew older, she'd warn me against falling into bad habits and 'letting myself go'. She'd seen women becoming so comfortable in their home environment – and so relaxed in their marriage – that they stopped making the effort, started to dress down every day and, as a result, just lost a little bit of self-respect. I know this is a very old-fashioned view that others might think belongs in the 1950s, but I think there's some truth in what Mam says. I don't see anything wrong in keeping up standards and making the best of yourself. I always feel better when I'm smartly dressed and wearing a touch of make-up.

My glamorous Granny Mary has had a big influence on me, too. Now ninety years old, she lives in her own trailer, next door to one of my aunts, and is still incredibly fashion-conscious. She adores her fur coats and designer handbags – with her broad American accent, she's got the air of an old Hollywood movie star – and she applies a full face of make-up every morning. She famously never lets her standards slip; even on the day of my grandad's funeral we spotted her constantly reapplying her make-up as she sat crying in the front pew of the church. Every couple of minutes, after dabbing her eyes, she'd produce her kohl eyeliner out of her handbag, expertly pencilling in a black line without any need for a mirror.

'Oh my God, she's putting her make up on,' I whispered to Tyson, trying very hard not to laugh. Giggling at a family funeral is never a good look.

'She probably wants to look her best for your grandad,' he replied. And he had a point. That's exactly how she'd have seen it.

My granny still looks amazing for her age – she defies nature – and, over the years, she's given me lots of beauty advice. When I was a young girl, she encouraged me to wash my face with very mild soap and water – 'it'll make your skin glow, Paris, and it won't strip it of its natural oils . . .' – and that's been my twice-daily ritual for the last two decades. It may seem really basic – and quite surprising coming from a former beautician, who's tried and tested all sorts of potions – but it works for me. I see no point in spending a fortune on expensive cleansing fluids when a bar of soap does the trick for a fraction of the price. My experience at college and in salons has shown me that costly products often promise more than they deliver – some cosmetics companies make very wild claims, and try to blind you with science – and, in my opinion, many of them just aren't worth the money. In the beauty world, it's often the case that 'less is more'.

Nevertheless, I think there are some decent skincare products that are worth a little extra investment. A good SPF moisturiser is a must-have, in my opinion (especially as you hit your thirties, when many skins begin to show signs of age) although I still don't believe it needs to cost the earth. There are some well-priced own-brand creams and lotions on the market that do the job brilliantly, often for less than a tenner. And while I love to sunbathe – I tan very easily – the fact I'm not blessed with a tropical climate in Morecambe means I always have a supply of fake tan to hand. I feel so much brighter with a sun-kissed complexion (clothes seem to look far better on me when I've got a golden glow, too) but I can only tolerate natural, hypoallergenic products as I'm prone to eczema flare-ups. After lots of trial and error I finally found myself a fabulous self-tanning mousse, which gets the occasional mention on my Instagram feed.

And while my visits to beauty salons and health spas are few and far between these days, I try to fit in the occasional treat. I adore a moisturising facial – I love how fresh and glowing your skin feels afterwards – and, if I need a bit of pampering, I'll book myself in for an aromatherapy back, neck and shoulder massage (which gives me a rare half-hour of total relaxation). I steer clear of any invasive or semi-invasive cosmetic procedures – so that's no lip fillers, cheek implants or chemical peels for me – but that's just my personal preference. The only cosmetic work I've had done took place in my mid-twenties, when I got my teeth straightened. As I'd got older they'd become a bit crooked, and whenever I was photographed or interviewed with Tyson I felt really self-conscious of my wonky smile. So I decided to book an appointment with a fantastic dentist who fitted me with an invisible brace for a few months. I was delighted with the end results; being able to smile with confidence again made such a difference.

I wouldn't deny anyone the right to improve and enhance their features – as I did with my teeth – but I think it's so important that any procedure is done safely, sensibly and appropriately. If someone is going to feel better about themselves by fixing their bumpy nose, or removing their unsightly mole, all power to them. But I do see the pressures people are under to opt for far more invasive surgery – especially young women – and it concerns me that it can so easily become addictive; a tweak here, an implant there, another lift elsewhere. It breaks my heart to see beautiful girls sometimes ruining their unique, God-given features in pursuit of what they believe is physical 'perfection'. And it makes me feel sad that they don't feel comfortable letting their natural beauty shine through. Perhaps they don't listen closely enough to those people who tell them they're lovely as they are, and that having procedure after procedure won't necessarily make them happier. That's certainly the message I'll be pressing home to my own children.

'Nobody's perfect, Paris, and there's always going to be somebody prettier out there,' my mam would say whenever I had moments of teenage insecurity. 'Be comfortable in your own skin. Be thankful for what you've got. The most important thing in life is that you're healthy and happy.'

And while I'm no Victoria's Secret model – I know my limitations – I think I've learned to make the most of myself with the right clothes and the right make-up, and I know I can turn on the glamour when I want to. But some days I look and feel better than others, like all of us. I have plenty of 'bad mirror mornings' – when I'm struggling to zip up my favourite jeans because I've had one too many doughnuts, perhaps, or my eyes look tired and puffy because I've been up all night with Adonis – but I try not to let it bother me too much. Over the years, particularly since I've had the kids, I've learned to accept my lumps and my bumps, and my faults and my flaws, and I'll just grab a roomier pair of jeans, or reach for my concealer, and get on with the rest of my day.

If I do find myself having a moan, however ('I'm getting chubby, Tyson . . . I'm missing those Fury Family work-outs . . .') my husband will give me a big kiss and tell me he loves me, whatever I look like. And he's being totally genuine when he says so. He's really sweet like that.

If there's one aspect of my appearance I've always been really self-conscious about, though, it's my fingernails. I'm a lifelong nail biter, I'm afraid to say, and every few weeks I have to get acrylics applied professionally to conceal the damage. I've been trying for years to kick the habit, but none of the remedies I've tried seem to work, including that foul-tasting liquid you can paint on. It's become a real problem; I've even been known to gnaw away at my brand new nails during nerve-shredding boxing matches.

'What on earth have you done to those beautiful creations?' my friend Cathy will say in the aftermath of a fight.

'I know, it's terrible . . .' I'll reply, hiding my tatty talons behind my back. 'I don't even realise I'm doing it.'

People may assume I spend hours titivating myself in beauty salons before one of Tyson's title fights, but they'd be wrong. Hair and make-up is the least of my worries during the build-up week, when Tyson is my priority and there's usually far too much going on to think about anything else. It's like having tunnel vision; it's all about the fight, and nothing else really matters. Only once have I ever booked myself into a swanky salon to get my hair washed, styled and curled – in Las Vegas, on the morning of the Deontay Wilder rematch – and I really regretted it. I emerged from the salon totally underwhelmed with the result – I knew I could've done a much better job myself – and, because I was so anxious about the looming fight, I hadn't really enjoyed all the fuss, bother and small-talk. I went straight back to my hotel room and restyled it myself.

Like most of the women in my family, I'm very lucky to have been blessed with a good head of hair. My long blond mane is my hallmark, I suppose, and it's become a source of fascination to many, because no one can believe it's all mine. It's unusually thick and coarse – I was once told by a hairdresser that I've got 'at least four heads' worth' – and, because of this, people assume I must be wearing weaves or extensions.

'Is your hair real, Paris?' is the question I'm asked most often (other than 'What's it like to be married to Tyson Fury, then?').

'Yes, it's one hundred per cent natural,' I'll reply, although judging by some raised eyebrows, I'm still not convinced everyone believes me. Sometimes I get the feeling they want to reach out and tug it just to double-check.

As for my hair colour, I'm naturally dark blond. I get it tinted at my local hair salon every six weeks or so, when I'll also get a quick trim and a few layers cut in. I avoid bleach at all costs. No matter what any stylist tells you, or what nourishing conditioner they try to flog you, hydrogen peroxide kills your hair. In the past I've made the mistake of going for a platinum blond look but, once I began a cycle of over-bleaching, I ended up with a frizzy mop that began snapping off left, right and centre. So now I steer clear, instead going for a more golden blond. I've dyed my hair brown a couple of times – including during lockdown, when I had a mishap with a cheap DIY colouring kit – but it just doesn't suit me at all.

I only wash my hair twice a week – I think it helps to preserve its natural oils – and I do my best to avoid blow-drying, so will try to let it dry naturally. I don't waste money on expensive shampoo and conditioner, and since my teenage years have used a very well-known French-sounding brand designed for colour-treated hair. I do treat myself to a couple of luxury products, though; one's a hair masque that I use every couple of weeks, the other's a heat-styling serum that I use before I straighten or curl my hair with tongs.

Someone once asked me what single cosmetic product I'd take onto a desert island, and I knew the answer straight away: a lifetime's supply of my cheap, supermarket-bought conditioner. My skin is tough enough to withstand the sun – I'd turn a nice chestnut brown – but there's no way my hair would survive. Without any moisture it would turn into a big ball of yellow straw. My sister-in-law Helen once had the misfortune of seeing me in all my unconditioned glory while on holiday, and coined a nickname that has stuck.

'Look who it is, it's the Lion King!' she said, bursting out laughing.

In May 2021, when I was about five months pregnant, Tyson flew to Las Vegas. He was in the process of buying a property over there, a lovely six-bedroom house in a nice part of town that the whole family could use whenever we visited. Tyson had spent a lot of time in the boxing capital of the world, and he thought it'd be a good idea to find a permanent base rather than having to stay in rented accommodation.

He'd also crossed the Atlantic to sort out a legal matter regarding Deontay Wilder. A date had been set for Tyson's much-anticipated fight against fellow Brit, Anthony Joshua – Saturday 14 August 2021 – but Wilder had mounted a challenge to it, claiming that Tyson was contractually obliged to fight him for a third time prior to any other bout taking place. If the Joshua fight were to proceed, he'd be seeking millions of pounds in compensation. Tyson's preference was to fight Joshua – he'd set his heart on this blockbuster bout, as had so many boxing fans around the world – but he was unwilling to stump up any cash to Wilder from his own purse. The final decision would rest with a judge, and Tyson just had to cross his fingers. He hoped he'd only need to stay in Vegas for three or four weeks in order to finalise both the legal matters and the house matters.

A fortnight before he jetted out to Vegas, and perhaps aware that my advancing pregnancy was starting to tire me a little, Tyson had run something by me.

'Why don't I take Prince over to America for a few weeks, Paris?' he'd asked. 'It'd give you a bit of a break. Four kids to look after instead of five. And he'd be great company for me.'

'Well, OK,' I'd replied, agreeing it might be a good idea in the circumstances. 'Just make sure you both stay safe.'

There were a couple of alternative scenarios for us to consider, though. If the court case went well and the house sale went through, Tyson would return home to the UK with Prince. That was Plan A. But if there were any setbacks, and he needed to extend his stay in Las Vegas, Plan B would see me flying out to America to collect my son. I could also then combine the trip with a late-spring holiday in Miami with the rest of the kids.

I didn't really have an issue with Prince spending some quality time with his dad, just as long as he caught up with his schoolwork when he got back home. So I packed my boys' suitcases, dropped them off at Manchester Airport and, for the next few weeks, kept in touch via phone or FaceTime. I scrolled through the photos on Tyson's Instagram timeline, too, to see what they were getting up to. While it was bucketing down with rain in Morecambe – it was the worst spring weather we'd had for years – father and son seemed to be having a blast in sunny Vegas, going on road trips together and enjoying meals out with Tyson's boxing buddies. Soon they'd jet across the country to Miami, with Tyson's brother Tommy in tow.

In mid-May, we received good and bad news. On the one hand, the house sale went through without any hitches. On the other hand, Tyson found out he'd lost the court case against Deontay Wilder. Since compensation wasn't on the table, the judge had ruled that a third fight against his American rival would have to take place, so it was quickly scheduled for Las Vegas on Saturday 24 July 2021. The bout with Anthony Joshua would have to be put on the back burner for the time being. Tyson was dismayed – at one point he'd thought things were going his way – but, credit to him, he sucked it up, switched his sights and set the wheels in motion, organising a two-month training camp in Vegas. He was more determined than ever to beat Wilder in the final part of their 'trilogy'; there was an extra bit of needle between them now.

'It is what it is, Paris,' said Tyson during a catch-up chat. 'I've just got to get on with it.'

'Yeah, time to stay positive,' I said. 'It's not ideal, but what can you do?'

I wouldn't be able to attend the big fight, of course. I'd be eight months pregnant by late July, and wouldn't be able to travel. I tried my best to hide my disappointment while on the phone to Tyson – I didn't want to further dampen his spirits – but he'd have probably known how low I was feeling. I'd only ever missed a couple of his fights – and that had been ages ago – and the prospect of not being there in person filled me with dread. Watching a boxing match from home was going to be far more stressful than witnessing it live, and I knew just how helpless I'd feel being so far away. Being part of Tyson's fight-night entourage had been an important ritual for both of us over the years, and cheering him on from the ringside, and being so close to the action, had always been a real comfort to me.

So, with Tyson unable to bring Prince home to the UK, I jetted over to America with the kids for a fortnight – our Plan B – and the seven of us were reunited in Miami. This time we stayed in a private villa, though, as we'd wanted to avoid a repeat of Christmas, when we'd hardly had a moment to ourselves. However, now that the media interest in Fury v Wilder III had gone into overdrive, the British tabloids set about trying to get any Tyson-related story they could, including a story about our marriage being in trouble that couldn't have been further from the truth. Everywhere we went as a family, from a trip to the Versace Mansion to a meal on Ocean Drive, we were followed by camera-clicking paparazzi. It was really frightening for the younger children – they often ended up in tears – and after a few days of this, we'd had enough. Tyson and I needed to get the media off our backs, once and for all, even if it meant giving them something to write about ourselves. So, one afternoon, Venezuela filmed a short video of us both at the villa, looking all loved up and larking around by the pool. It wasn't an act; we were genuinely feeling happy with life and were having lots of fun in the sun. Tyson added a caption ('Pregnant wife time ... reunited ...') and uploaded the footage to Instagram.

'Did you really have to send that to the whole world, Tyson?' I moaned. 'Who wants to see pictures of me and my great big bump in a bikini?'

'It might just give us a bit of breathing space,' he said. 'And anyway, you and the bump look beautiful.'

It seemed to do the trick. Within hours, screenshots of the video appeared on countless online news sites and the press attention began to gradually fade away, thank goodness.

During a family meal at Sugar Factory – a famous ice cream and dessert restaurant in Miami Beach that the kids were desperate to visit – Tyson brought up the subject of Baby #6. He came up with the idea that I should stay put in America for the entire spring and summer, so I could give birth in Las Vegas instead of going back home to the UK. He suggested that me and the kids could live in the new house while he was in the boxing camp – he'd stop in the property he usually rented – and by the time the fight had taken place, my due date would only be a few weeks away.

Back at the villa I toyed with the idea – it was tempting, I must admit – but I soon concluded there was little logic to it. First and foremost, I had a pretty bad medical history with my final stage of pregnancies – the condition I suffered with, cholestasis, had led to all my births being induced – and I didn't like the idea of being in an unfamiliar hospital that had never had me as a patient. Also, other than the kids, I'd be pretty much home alone in Vegas most of the time. Tyson would hardly be on the scene because he'd be locked away in his training camp and, due to the unpredictable coronavirus situation, I doubted I'd be able to fly over any family members to help in his absence.

'It just wouldn't work out,' I said to Tyson as we talked things through again. 'I need to be at home.'

'I understand, Paris,' he said. 'I just hate the idea of being apart from you for so long.'

Saying goodbye to Tyson at Miami airport was incredibly emotional. We'd had a lovely fortnight together as a family, and as he and I hugged and kissed we fully expected not to get to see each other for three long months. Parting company was difficult at the best of times, but I was now returning to Morecambe conscious that I'd be missing my husband's big fight, and – more upsettingly – that I'd be going through the later stages of pregnancy without him by my side. God willing, my only hope was he'd be back home in plenty of time for the birth itself in August. He promised me he'd be on the first flight out of Las Vegas following the Wilder fight, and that nothing and nobody would stop him. Welcoming a newborn into the world was one of those special moments in life, and we wanted to share it together.

If I'm ever asked to reveal the secret of my long-ish marriage to Tyson, there's always one word at the top of my list: friendship. I think it's the bedrock of any enduring relationship. When you start seeing someone, you're carried away in that whirlwind of passion and excitement – the first kiss, the hot dates – and you find yourselves walking around in a loved-up daze. But when that intensity starts to drop – which inevitably happens when you settle into the routine of married life, and the babies come along – you'll find your-selves relying more on your deep friendship to bond you together. For things to work, you need to get along well. You need to actually *like* one another. I know that may sound completely obvious, but I've seen a few couples fall by the wayside when they've realised, once the love-fest is over, the underlying friendship just isn't there.

And while you don't always need to have matching person-alities – opposites can attract, of course – I think a good rela-tionship needs lots of common ground. Compatibility is important. Tyson and I are different in many ways – he's more emotional and intense, I'd say, and I'm much more practical and easy-going – but we're definitely on the same wavelength when it comes to our likes and dislikes, and our interests and pastimes. We share a similar sense of humour – it's got us through the bleakest of times – and if we're not being daft and making each other laugh, we're giggling at movies like *Dumb and Dumber* and *Knocked Up*.

Like many couples, we like chilling out in front of the TV; on a Friday night we'll put the younger kids to bed and curl up on the sofa together to watch *Game of Thrones* or *The Rain.* We like the same kind of music (we're both big fans of Chris Stapleton and Patsy Cline) and we love a good sing-along at home or in the car (it's not just Tyson who can carry a tune, as it happens). If there's no training camp taking place, our ideal weekend is spent either walking in the outdoors with the children – in the hills, or along the beach

– or organising a get-together for friends and family. Quality time with our nearest and dearest is everything.

To me, sharing special moments and making precious memories is what marriage is all about. Whether it's been witnessing our babies' first steps, going on sightseeing holidays or having merry family Christmases, it's those common experiences that make your relationship so rich and worthwhile. When Tyson and I reach old age, I don't think we'll be sat on our decking, in our rocking chairs, reminiscing about all the flash cars and fancy jewellery we bought over the years. I'd like to think we'll be casting our minds back to all those happy family times we enjoyed together as man and wife, surrounded by our lovely kids.

Our shared Traveller background has acted as a glue throughout our married life, too. It has given us a belief system that not only encourages us to worship God – our faith is very important to us – but also inspires us to raise our children to respect the core family values we hold so dear, like kindness and consideration. As parents, Tyson and I are committed to bringing up our sons and daughters to become decent, hard-working, down-to-earth people, even though they've been born into great wealth and privilege. We don't want to raise a bunch of spoilt, entitled little brats. We want them to appreciate what they have, but to also understand that fame and money doesn't guarantee happiness – the opposite can be the case, as their dad will testify – and that the simpler things in life can often have more meaning. I hope it's a good sign that my kids are equally excited by a week spent on a Traveller site in the Midlands as they are a fortnight spent in Miami.

'Guess where we're going on Friday, kids,' I'll say.

'Is it Granny's?' they'll reply. '*Please* say it's Granny's . . .'

And while Tyson and I may not have as much time for romance nowadays, there are ways to rekindle the spark and keep the flame burning. We still have our wonderful moments – an occasional weekend break, a cosy candlelit meal or a gift-wrapped little something – which prevents us getting into that dreaded rut. Rare though they are, we love our date nights and always make the most of them, putting on our favourite designer outfits and heading over to a nice restaurant in Manchester or Liverpool. Like most couples with kids, Tyson and I will promise not to spend our entire evening talking about the children but it often ends up that way – inevitably so, perhaps, because so much of our life revolves around them. But, whatever the subject matter, being alone in each other's company is always so special. It reminds us why we got together in the first place, and how well we get on. We are, as Tyson says, each other's Number One Fan.

Staying with the same person for so long, not to mention marrying young and having children early, was never going to be a walk in the park. It's needed a great deal of hard work from both parties to keep it afloat, including lots of patience, compromise and understanding. Like many other long-standing couples, our relationship has had its high spots and its low points, with a few rough-ish patches in between. We've gone through some turbulent times as husband and wife, from baby loss to severe depression, but, together, we've always pulled ourselves through it. We've hung on in there. We've stuck at it. We've never thrown in the towel, as they say in boxing.

I still vividly remember something Mam told me a few years back. Tyson was slowly but surely emerging from his worst bout of depression, and I was beginning to pick up the pieces, trying to work out exactly how our marriage had survived intact.

'There's a reason why you two will always make it through, Paris,' she said. 'You love him, and he loves you. Sometimes it's as simple as that.'

So what does the future hold for us Furys? As for Tyson's boxing career, I think he has three or four big fights left in him yet, which means he'll probably retire in his mid-thirties. If it was up to me, however, I'd prefer him to call it quits sooner rather than later. Watching him slug it out against hard-hitting opponents doesn't get any easier for me – I can't bear the thought of him getting badly hurt, and I'm petrified that one punch might change everything in an instant. But I understand why he wants to carry on for a few years. This isn't about money or fame; he doesn't need any more of either. It's about desire and ambition. At this point in time Tyson feels so mentally and physically strong, and while that remains the case he sees no reason to step out of the ring. He believes he still has a great deal to offer his beloved sport, and lots more to achieve.

'But haven't you done enough to put your name in the history books?' I'll ask him, even though I know what his answer will be. 'Why carry on, and put yourself at risk?'

'Because I've still got that hunger, that determination,' he'll say. 'I'll know when my time's up, Paris, don't you worry. It's just not right now.'

Whatever happens with his boxing, though, I'll still be in the thick of it. For as long as he fights professionally, I'll always play my part in Team Fury, and will continue to take my prime position at ringside so I can cheer him on and send positive vibes. I can't ever imagine taking a back seat. Boxing is ingrained in my DNA, whether I like it or not, and I just have to be involved, to be on the scene. And even though I have a love/hate relationship with the sport – it's brought me pain as well as joy – I know I'll miss it badly when it's gone.

Even though it may be a few years down the line, Tyson and I have discussed his life after boxing. I used to really worry how he'd manage to fill that huge void, and whether anything else could possibly compete, but as time has gone on I've become far more optimistic. Tyson is much more in control of his life nowadays – and a lot happier in his own skin – and, as a result, his outlook has never been so positive and upbeat. He has his good days and bad days but – touch wood – since his 2018 comeback there haven't been any continuous, lingering stretches of mental ill-health. Tyson knows the black cloud of depression will never vanish completely – it'll always be hovering on the horizon, threatening to drift overhead – but, by putting strategies in place, he has learned to control it and keep it at bay. Regular training and exercise has been his salvation – the boxing gym is his happy place – as has his devotion to his faith and his family. They continue to be his priorities in life, and they will always spur him on and keep him focused.

So as things stand, it looks like Tyson will progress into coaching when his boxing career draws to a close. He and his trainer, SugarHill Steward, have already discussed the possibility of going into business together, as they're both equally keen to discover and nurture promising new talent on both sides of the Atlantic. Tyson has already had a taste of this with the young boxers who use his gym in Morecambe, who'll often ask him for advice and guidance. He loves the idea of passing on his knowledge and experience to the next generation of fighters, and I think he'd love to train a future heavyweight champion of the world. Knowing Tyson as I do, I think it'd give him as much pleasure and satisfaction as winning his own title belts.

I'm often asked if my kids will follow in their dad's footsteps and become boxers. It wouldn't surprise me if one or two of them did, since they've grown up around the sport and it's become such a huge part of their lives. If they did, though, I know it'd be ten times more stressful than watching Tyson. Those maternal instincts of mine would take over and, if I sensed they were in trouble, I'd be like a lioness protecting her cubs. I could see myself climbing through the ropes and rushing to their aid.

'Mam, what are you doing . . . you're embarrassing me.'

'Getting you out of this ring, that's what . . .'

But ultimately it's their choice whether they go into boxing. While me and Tyson don't go out of our way to encourage them – there's no pressure from us whatsoever – we don't discourage them, either. We just tell our kids we'll support them whichever path they choose, whether it's going down the sport route, the business route or (like me) the child-rearing route. They all have equal merit, as far as I'm concerned. When it comes down to it, we just want our sons and daughters to be happy and healthy and, as they become adults themselves, to find loving relationships and raise families of their own. I hope they'll get the same joy out of parenting that I have over the years. When the time comes, Granny Paris will always be on hand to help out with their childcare, of course, just like my lovely mam has always done with me.

So far Tyson and I have both packed a lot into our thirty-something years on this planet – there's never been a dull moment with the Furys, that's for sure – but we've still got plenty of living left to do, plenty of places we want to visit, and plenty of people we want to meet. Although sunny Morecambe will be our base for the foreseeable future, when Tyson finally hangs up his gloves we definitely plan to spend more time abroad, in Europe or America, perhaps, maybe even further afield. But as long as we're together, collecting those precious memories, I'll be happy wherever we end up.

'It doesn't matter where you're going,' someone once told me, 'it's who you have beside you.'

ACKNOWLEDGEMENTS

FIRSTLY, I WANT to pay tribute to my mother Lynda, who raised me to be stronger than I ever thought I'd have to be. She has always done her very best for my brother, my sisters and me, and has helped out our family more times than I can count. And what is a woman without her friends? My sister Montana, my aunt Romain and Shannon and Cathy have always listened to me and offered their support when needed, and I thank them all so much.

As for making this book possible, I'm very grateful to the brilliant team at Hodder & Stoughton, especially Rowena Webb, who believed I had a good tale to tell and encouraged and guided me though the whole process. I also want to thank Joanne Lake for piecing together my crazy life story. We spent hour after hour and day after day putting all my thoughts and memories into some kind of order, and I'm so proud of what we've created.

PICTURE ACKNOWLEDGEMENTS

Inset 1

Pages 1–6: © Paris Fury

Page 7, top: © Shutterstock; middle: © Reuters / Ina Fassbender; bottom: © Marianne Mueller/Anadolu Agency/ Getty Images

Page 8, top: © PA Photos / TopFoto; bottom: © Paris Fury

Inset 2

Page 1, top left and right: © Paris Fury; bottom: © OLI SCARFF/AFP via Getty Images

Page 2: © Paris Fury

Page 3, top: © Kohjiro Kinno / Sports Illustrated via Getty Images; bottom left: © Mark J Terrill/AP/Shutterstock; bottom right: © Paris Fury

Page 4, top: © Paris Fury; middle: © REUTERS/Steve Marcus; bottom: © REUTERS/Steve Marcus

Page 5, top: © Paris Fury; bottom left and right: © Paris Fury

Page 6: © Paris Fury

Page 7, top: © Paris Fury; middle: © Al Bello/Getty Images; bottom: © Al Bello/Getty Images
Page 8, top: © Ken McKay/ITV/Shutterstock; middle: © ITV/Shutterstock; bottom left: © Paris Fury